JAMES DOUGLAS

Stop Saying Sorry

How to Break the Habit of Apologizing Your Life Away

Applebee Press

Contents

Introduction

Why We Can't Stop Saying Sorry

Have you ever caught yourself saying "sorry" before you even knew what you were apologizing for? Maybe it was when someone bumped into you at the grocery store and you instinctively blurted it out—even though they were the one steering the cart into your side. Or maybe it was in an email at work: *Sorry to bother you, just wondering if you had a chance to look at that report.* Maybe you said it when a friend called while you were busy, or when you started to cry, or when you simply dared to take up space.

If this sounds familiar, you're not alone. Over-apologizing is such a common reflex that many of us don't even notice how often we do it. We say "sorry" for being late, for asking a question, for needing help, for existing in a way that might inconvenience someone else. For many, especially women, it's practically stitched into our vocabulary. And while a well-placed, heartfelt apology is one of the most powerful ways to repair trust, reflexive apologies do the opposite: they chip away at our confidence, our authority, and sometimes even our relationships.

But here's the truth: over-apologizing isn't a character flaw. It's not proof that you're weak, needy, or broken. It's a safety strategy. Somewhere along the way, your nervous system learned that shrinking yourself, smoothing things over, and preemptively taking the blame kept you safe—safe from rejection, conflict, punishment, or even just uncomfortable silence. "Sorry" became your shield.

This book is here to help you lay that shield down. Not by swinging to the other extreme and refusing to apologize when you truly should—but by learning the difference between real accountability and needless self-blame. Together, we'll explore why the "sorry reflex" shows up, how it holds you back, and— most importantly—how to replace it with words and actions that reflect your true strength. You'll find practical tools, scripts, and small daily practices that help you shift from reflexive apology to confident, authentic communication.

So, take a breath. You don't have to apologize for reading this book, for wanting to grow, or for finally saying: *enough is enough*. By the end, you'll not only know how to stop saying sorry all the time—you'll know how to live unapologetically.

1

The Sorry Reflex

If you kept a little clicker in your pocket and tallied every time you said "sorry" today, what number would you end up with? Five? Ten? Twenty?

For many of us, the count would be shockingly high. We apologize when we bump into someone, when we speak up in a meeting, when we take too long to text back, when we can't make it to a friend's birthday dinner, or when our toddler melts down in public. We even apologize for things we can't possibly control—like the rain ruining a picnic or the Wi-Fi cutting out on a video call.

That's what I call the **"sorry reflex."** It's a quick, automatic, almost unconscious reaction. Like a hiccup of the mouth. Before you've even registered what happened, the word slips out: *sorry*.

At first glance, it seems harmless—just good manners, right? But over time, this reflex can become a script that governs your relationships, your workplace presence, and your self-esteem. Let's unpack what it looks like, why it happens, and what it's really costing you.

Recognizing the Habit

The tricky thing about the sorry reflex is that it hides in plain sight. You may not even notice how often you're doing it, because it's woven into the fabric of everyday speech.

Think about these scenarios:

- You ask a barista for oat milk instead of almond and immediately tack on, "Sorry about that!" as if your coffee order were a personal inconvenience.
- You slip into a crowded elevator and mumble "sorry" to every single person you pass—even though you have as much right to the space as they do.
- A colleague interrupts you in a meeting, and your instinct is to apologize: "Oh, sorry—go ahead."
- Your child needs help with homework, and you start with, "Sorry, I was just finishing an email," even though tending to both things is perfectly normal.

These little moments seem insignificant, but they add up. Each "sorry" sends a subtle message—not just to the world, but to your own nervous system—that you are a disruption. That you are wrong for needing, asking, taking, speaking, or simply being.

And once it's ingrained, the reflex shows up everywhere. You'll see it in your texts ("Sorry, just saw this!"), your emails ("Sorry to follow up..."), your apologies for things outside your control ("Sorry the traffic was bad"), and even in your physical presence: the way you shrink into yourself on the subway or slide your chair back too far in a meeting so you don't take up "too much space."

The first step to breaking the reflex is noticing it. Try this: for one day, write down every single time you say "sorry." Don't judge it yet. Don't try to change it. Just record. You'll be surprised at how often it sneaks into places you didn't even realize.

The Cost of Over-Apologizing

Now, you might be thinking: *But isn't it better to be overly polite than rude? Isn't saying sorry just being nice?*

Yes—sometimes. A genuine, well-placed apology is one of the most powerful tools for connection and repair we have. But when "sorry" becomes your default, it loses its meaning. And worse—it chips away at your confidence and credibility.

Here's what it costs you:

1. It undermines your authority.

In professional settings, especially, constant apologies can make you sound uncertain—even when you're fully competent. Compare these two statements:

- "Sorry, I just had a quick question about the budget."
- "I have a question about the budget."

The first makes it sound like your question is an intrusion. The second communicates clarity, curiosity, and confidence. The difference is only one word, but it changes how others perceive you.

2. It dilutes real apologies.

When every interaction includes an "I'm sorry," the words lose power. If you apologize for spilling coffee on someone *and* for asking them to hand you a pen, the other person doesn't know which situations truly warrant repair. Over time, your apologies may start to sound insincere—even when you mean them.

3. It keeps you small.

Each reflexive sorry reinforces the belief that you're at fault for existing in ways that take up space. It's like repeatedly telling yourself, "You don't belong." That internal script doesn't just affect your words—it shapes your posture, your willingness to speak up, and the way you show up in relationships.

And perhaps the most painful cost? Resentment. When you're constantly apologizing for things you shouldn't be, you often end up feeling resentful—at yourself for shrinking, at others for not noticing your sacrifice, and at the world for being so quick to accept your guilt.

The First Step: Awareness

Before you can stop the sorry reflex, you have to learn how it operates in your daily life. Here are a few simple awareness practices to begin:

1. Track your "sorry triggers."

Carry a small notebook or use your phone to jot down when and where you catch yourself apologizing. Do certain situations (work, family, social media) trigger more sorries than others?

2. Listen to your body.

The reflex often starts as a physical sensation—tightness in your chest, nervous laughter, a shrinking of your shoulders—before the word slips out. Notice these cues. They're your nervous system sounding the alarm.

3. Journal your reflections.

At the end of the day, look back at your apology log. Which

sorries felt necessary? Which felt automatic? Which surprised you? The goal here isn't to judge yourself—it's to build a map of your reflex.

Think of this as detective work. You're gathering clues about your own habits. By shining a light on the reflex, you remove some of its power. You start to see that "sorry" isn't who you are—it's just something you've practiced so long, it feels natural.

Closing Thought for Chapter 1:

The sorry reflex didn't come out of nowhere. It has roots in culture, family, and nervous-system survival strategies. In the next chapter, we'll explore *why* you learned to apologize so often—and why your brain thinks it's keeping you safe by doing so. But for now, take a breath. If your notebook is already full of tally marks, don't panic. This isn't about shaming yourself for saying sorry. It's about noticing. Awareness is the first step toward change.

2

Why We Apologize Too Much

Have you ever wondered *why* your mouth seems to move faster than your brain when you say "sorry"? Before you even register what happened, the apology is already out there, floating in the air. Sometimes you don't even mean it—yet it feels almost dangerous not to say it.

That's because over-apologizing isn't just a bad habit. It has roots: cultural, psychological, and even biological. To unlearn it, we first need to understand where it came from.

Let's peel back the layers.

The Survival Story in Your Nervous System

Imagine your nervous system as a security guard. Its number-one job is to keep you safe. When it senses a threat—whether that's a lion in the savannah or your boss's raised eyebrow—it flips into protection mode. You've probably heard of the big three responses: **fight, flight, or freeze.** But there's a fourth one that doesn't get as much attention: **fawn.**

Fawning is the instinct to appease, to smooth things over, to make yourself as agreeable as possible so the "threat" doesn't explode. It's your nervous system whispering, *If I can keep this person happy, I'll be safe.*

Now, you probably don't have saber-toothed tigers lurking in your backyard. But your body doesn't know the difference between physical danger and emotional danger. A sharp tone of voice, a frown, or even silence from someone you care about can trigger that same fawn reflex. And the fastest way to fawn? A quick, "sorry."

Think about a child who learns that the only way to calm an angry parent is to apologize—even if they don't know what they did wrong. That child grows up believing that saying sorry equals safety. By adulthood, the nervous system is so well-trained in this move that the word just spills out.

So if you've been frustrated with yourself for apologizing too much, take a breath. You weren't weak—you were wired.

The Cultural Scripts We Inherit

Beyond biology, culture plays a huge role in how often we apologize. Some cultures encourage directness; others prize politeness and deference. But across many societies, one pattern is especially loud: **women are expected to apologize more than men.**

Studies show that women report saying sorry more often—not because they feel guiltier, but because they perceive more of their everyday actions as "offenses." Taking up time in a meeting, asking for help, even expressing an opinion can all feel like they warrant an apology. From an early age, girls are praised for being "nice," "agreeable," and "easy to get along with." Apologizing becomes shorthand for being good.

Maybe you remember being told as a child to "say you're sorry" even when your sibling was clearly at fault, just to keep the peace. Or maybe you absorbed the idea that good daughters, good students, good friends don't make waves.

Layer on top of that the messages we get from media: the sitcom character who over-apologizes for comic relief, the rom-com heroine who stumbles and says "sorry" in a flustered, lovable way, the endless ads selling products by highlighting flaws we didn't even know we should be sorry for.

It's no wonder so many of us grow into adults whose tongues are trained to lead with apology.

Family Dynamics and Early Lessons

If culture sets the stage, family writes the first script.

- Maybe you grew up in a household where tension crackled like static in the air, and you learned that smoothing things over with an apology could keep the peace.
- Maybe you were the eldest child, carrying the unspoken job of caretaker, keeping siblings out of trouble and parents calm. "Sorry" became part of your toolkit for survival.
- Or maybe your family valued appearances above all—so even small missteps had to be quickly glossed over with an apology, whether you meant it or not.

These early lessons are powerful. A child doesn't just learn *when* to say sorry; they learn *who* they are in the family story: the peacekeeper, the responsible one, the "good kid." And once those roles harden, it's hard to let them go.

One client I worked with described her role as "the sponge."

She absorbed every bit of family tension—anger, sadness, disappointment—and tried to soak it up before anyone else got wet. Her go-to phrase was "sorry"—a tiny, desperate attempt to wring out the chaos. Decades later, she was still saying sorry in meetings, on dates, at the grocery store checkout. The reflex had followed her, long past its usefulness.

Exercises: Uncovering Your Why

Now that we've pulled back the curtain, let's make this personal. You don't just over-apologize in the abstract—you do it for reasons that are uniquely yours. Try these short reflections:

1. Your First Memories of Sorry

- Can you remember the first time someone told you to say you were sorry?
- Was it a situation where you truly felt regret—or one where you were just told it was the "right" thing to do?
- What did you learn about yourself from that moment?

2. The Roles You Played

- Were you the peacekeeper, the overachiever, the comedian, the "easy kid"?
- How did apologies fit into that role?
- Which of those patterns are still showing up in your adult life?

3. The Safety Link

- Think of a time you apologized when you didn't need to.

- What did your body feel in that moment—tight chest, racing heart, knot in your stomach?
- What did you fear would happen if you didn't apologize?

Writing these reflections down—even just a few bullet points—can help you spot the old rules running your life.

Closing Thought for Chapter 2

When you find yourself over-apologizing, remember: you didn't choose this reflex in a vacuum. It was shaped by your body's survival instincts, your culture's expectations, and your family's early lessons. In other words: there's nothing "wrong" with you.

But here's the good news: once you understand where it came from, you can begin to unlearn it. You can start to rewrite the scripts.

In the next chapter, we'll explore the psychology of "sorry" even more deeply—how anxiety, perfectionism, and people-pleasing fuel this habit, and why letting go of it can feel so terrifying at first.

For now, give yourself credit: the fact that you're reading this means you're ready to understand your reflex instead of simply living inside it. That awareness is the beginning of change.

3

The Psychology of Sorry

By now, you know that over-apologizing isn't just politeness gone too far—it's a reflex rooted in your nervous system, your culture, and your earliest family roles. But there's another layer to this story: what's happening in your mind and emotions every time "sorry" leaps out.

Over-apologizing is often tangled up with anxiety, perfectionism, and people-pleasing. In other words, "sorry" isn't just a word—it's a psychological strategy. It's the brain's way of saying: *If I can soften this moment, maybe I'll avoid the pain I fear is coming.*

Let's dig into the psychology beneath the reflex and see why it feels so urgent—and so hard to stop.

The Fawn Response: Sorry as Survival

We touched on the fawn response earlier, but it's worth slowing down here. While fight, flight, and freeze get most of the attention, fawning is just as powerful. It's the urge to immediately soothe, pacify, and please in the face of perceived danger.

Imagine being at work, and your manager frowns at an email you sent. Even before they say a word, you feel your stomach flip. Your nervous system whispers: *Make it right. Smooth this over. Show them you're harmless.* And the word that jumps out? "Sorry."

The tricky part is that fawning *works*—at least temporarily. That's why your brain keeps using it. When you say sorry, you may notice the tension drop slightly in the room. The conflict seems to ease. You feel a little safer. But that safety is fragile, and the cost is high. You've reinforced the idea that your worth depends on others' approval and your ability to preemptively fix things.

Over time, this wires your brain to expect rejection if you don't apologize—even when no one is upset. It's not just a habit. It's a conditioned survival strategy.

Anxiety, Perfectionism, and the Apology Loop

Let's talk about anxiety. For many people, "sorry" becomes a way to manage the constant hum of *What if I've done something wrong? What if they're upset with me? What if I'm not enough?*

Anxiety thrives on "what if." Apologies are like little fire extinguishers you carry around, ready to spray at the first sign of smoke—even if there's no fire. They give the illusion of control: *If I say sorry, maybe I can stop the bad thing from happening.*

Perfectionism plays into this too. If you're someone who holds yourself to impossibly high standards, every small misstep feels like a major failure. Being one minute late? Catastrophe. Forgetting to send an attachment? Disaster. The quickest way to clean it up? Apologize—often excessively.

But here's the trap: anxiety and perfectionism don't actually get soothed by more apologies. In fact, the more you apologize, the more your brain links *relief* to *sorry.* So it keeps sending the urge, and the cycle continues.

- **Anxiety says:** "Something's wrong."
- **Perfectionism adds:** "And it's your fault."
- **The sorry reflex answers:** "I'll fix it by apologizing."
- **Relief comes—temporarily.**
- **Cycle resets.**

It's like scratching a mosquito bite: it feels better for a moment, but the itch comes back stronger.

Sorry as Self-Soothing

Here's a surprising truth: sometimes you're not even apologizing for the other person—you're apologizing to calm *yourself.*

Think about the last time you blurted out an unnecessary sorry. Did it feel like a little exhale? A release of tension? That's because over-apologizing doubles as an emotional regulation tool. Your nervous system believes that saying sorry reduces danger, so your body relaxes—at least for a moment.

But the relief is shallow. Instead of genuinely soothing yourself (through deep breathing, grounding, or honest self-talk), you outsource the job to another person's response. You feel okay only if they smile, say "no problem," or reassure you. If they don't? The anxiety spikes all over again.

This creates a dependency loop: your calm depends on someone else's reaction. And that's exhausting.

A Case Story: Marissa's Meetings

Marissa was a bright, capable project manager in her thirties. But every time she ran a team meeting, she started with the same phrase: "Sorry, I just want to go over a few things."

Her colleagues noticed. Some shrugged it off. Others began to see her as less confident, less authoritative. What Marissa didn't realize was that her constant apologies were sending a silent message: *I'm not sure I belong here.*

When we dug deeper, we found that Marissa's "sorry" wasn't really about her team. It was about her anxiety. She felt a rush of nervous energy every time she addressed a group. The word "sorry" acted like a little pressure valve, letting some of that steam escape. But it also undercut her credibility.

Once she saw this pattern, she began practicing a swap. Instead of "Sorry, I just want to go over a few things," she tried: "Let's start by reviewing today's agenda." Simple. Clear. Confident.

It wasn't easy. Her nervous system still craved the soothing comfort of "sorry." But with practice, she began to feel that same sense of relief—not from apologizing, but from owning her space.

Exercises: Untangling the Psychology of Sorry

If you want to understand your own "why," here are a few exercises to try:

1. The Anxiety Inventory

- Write down situations where you feel a strong urge to apologize.

- Note what thoughts race through your mind: *They'll be mad. They'll think I'm rude. They'll leave me.*
- Ask: Is this fear about the actual situation—or about your anxiety projecting worst-case scenarios?

2. The Perfectionism Check

- Think of a time you apologized for something small, like sending an email late.
- Ask: What standard was I holding myself to? Was it realistic?
- How would I respond if someone else made the same "mistake"?

3. The Self-Soothing Swap

- Next time you feel the urge to say sorry, pause.
- Try a grounding technique instead: take three deep breaths, plant your feet firmly on the ground, or silently remind yourself, *I am safe. I don't need to apologize to be okay.*
- Notice how it feels to calm yourself without using "sorry" as the tool.

Closing Thought for Chapter 3

Over-apologizing is more than a bad habit—it's a psychological loop, powered by anxiety, perfectionism, and the need for self-soothing. It makes sense why your brain chose this strategy. It gave you relief. It helped you survive.

But survival isn't the same as thriving. To truly step out of the sorry reflex, you'll need new tools for managing anxiety, tolerating imperfection, and soothing yourself in healthy ways.

In the next chapter, we'll explore how all these hidden forces show up in your daily life—and how they affect not only you, but the people around you. We'll look at the social impact of over-apologizing, from careers to friendships to love. Because saying sorry too much doesn't just change how you feel—it changes how others see you.

4

The Social Impact of Sorry

It's one thing to recognize the sorry reflex in yourself. It's another to see how it ripples outward, shaping the way others perceive you and the way you show up in relationships. Every unnecessary apology sends a subtle message—not just about the moment, but about *you*. And over time, those messages add up.

Apologies can change how people view your competence, your confidence, and even your value in both personal and professional settings. They can alter power dynamics in relationships, and sometimes, they quietly erode your self-esteem. Let's take a closer look at how constant "sorry" lands in the world around you—and why it's worth learning to choose your apologies wisely.

Undermining Credibility

Picture two people in a meeting. Both are smart, prepared, and ready to share their ideas. The first begins:

"Sorry, I just wanted to add something. I don't know if this is helpful, but maybe we could try..."

The second says:

"I'd like to suggest an approach that might improve our results."

Same intention. Same idea. But which one do you trust more? Who sounds like they belong at the table?

This is the cost of the constant "sorry." It undermines credibility. Even when you *do* have expertise, your words come wrapped in doubt. Instead of seeing you as confident and capable, people may perceive you as tentative, insecure, or less knowledgeable than you actually are.

It doesn't help that research confirms this bias: leaders who hedge with excessive apologies or qualifiers are often rated as less competent, even when their ideas are strong. And unfortunately, women and marginalized voices tend to be judged more harshly in this arena, meaning the cost of a "sorry" can be even greater.

This doesn't mean you need to bulldoze into every room with bravado. But it does mean that a reflexive "sorry" can quietly chip away at the authority you've worked hard to build.

Relationship Strains

Now let's move from the workplace to our most personal spaces: our relationships. Over-apologizing here creates its own set of dynamics.

Take romantic partnerships. Imagine your partner accidentally leaves dishes in the sink, and you say: "Sorry, I should've reminded you earlier." Or they're running late, and you blurt: "Sorry, I didn't plan dinner better."

Over time, this creates an imbalance. You become the one

absorbing blame for ordinary life messiness, which can lead to frustration for both of you. Your partner may start expecting you to take responsibility for everything—or worse, they may stop taking accountability themselves because you're already doing it.

In friendships, constant "sorry" can create distance. If every canceled plan, delayed text, or honest mistake is met with an over-the-top apology, friends may start to feel uncomfortable or even guilty. They might think: *Do they really believe they've hurt me that badly? Or do they just not believe they're allowed to slip up?*

Here's the paradox: the more you apologize to keep relationships smooth, the more strain you may actually create.

The Self-Esteem Cycle

Perhaps the deepest impact of over-apologizing isn't external at all—it's internal. Every unnecessary sorry reinforces a story about who you are.

- *Sorry I took up your time* → I'm not worth the space I take.
- *Sorry for asking a question* → My curiosity is a burden.
- *Sorry for bothering you* → My needs are an inconvenience.

Say those things enough times, and you start to believe them. Your self-esteem erodes, not because the world told you you're unworthy, but because *you kept telling yourself that story with every apology.*

Low self-esteem then feeds back into the reflex. When you believe you're small, you act small. And when you act small, you apologize even more. The cycle tightens, until "sorry" feels like both the cause and the cure for the discomfort you carry.

A Case Story: Daniel at Work

Daniel was a talented graphic designer. His clients loved his work, but his boss often questioned his confidence. Why? Because Daniel's emails were filled with apologies.

"Sorry this is late" (it wasn't).

"Sorry if this isn't quite what you wanted" (it was exactly what they asked for).

"Sorry to bother you" (he was literally doing his job).

Daniel's boss started to wonder if he *really* knew what he was doing. In truth, Daniel was highly skilled. But the repeated apologies painted a picture of someone unsure, even though his work proved otherwise.

Once Daniel began stripping the "sorry" from his emails, something shifted. He didn't suddenly become arrogant or cold—he simply came across as clear and capable. His boss noticed. So did his clients. Nothing about his actual work changed—just the way he framed himself. And that made all the difference.

Exercises: Seeing the Impact

Understanding how others perceive your apologies can be eye-opening. Try these exercises to see the ripple effect more clearly:

1. The Two-Sentence Swap

- Write down a recent sentence where you used "sorry."
- Rewrite it without the apology.
- Read both out loud. Notice how the second one lands

differently—even in your own ears.

2. Ask a Trusted Friend

- Choose someone who knows you well.
- Ask them: "Do I apologize more than I need to? How does it come across?"
- Listen with curiosity, not defensiveness. Sometimes an outside perspective reveals patterns you can't see.

3. Notice the Reaction

- The next time you resist the urge to apologize, pay attention to how people respond.
- Do they seem offended—or do they simply accept your statement as it is?
- Record what happens. Often, you'll find the world doesn't crumble without your "sorry."

Closing Thought for Chapter 4

Over-apologizing doesn't just live inside you—it echoes in every space you enter. It changes how people perceive you, how relationships function, and how you view yourself. That doesn't mean you're doomed. It means you have enormous power to shift the story by changing just one word.

When you replace "sorry" with confident, clear, respectful communication, you don't lose kindness—you gain authenticity. People begin to see you not as the apologetic one, but as the capable, grounded, trustworthy one. And most importantly, *you begin to see yourself that way too.*

In the next chapter, we'll get even more personal. We'll look at the patterns that fuel your "sorry"—the specific situations, triggers, and roles you've adopted over the years. Because awareness of the impact is step one. Awareness of your unique patterns? That's step two.

5

Spotting Your Patterns

By now, you know that over-apologizing has deep roots—in your nervous system, your culture, your family, and your psychology. But to truly shift the reflex, you need to understand how it plays out in *your* everyday life. Where does "sorry" show up most often for you? What roles and triggers keep pulling you back into the habit?

This chapter is about becoming your own detective. You'll learn how to notice your specific patterns, decode the situations that make you most vulnerable to over-apologizing, and begin to separate real accountability from unnecessary self-blame.

Language Habits: The Words That Give You Away

Let's start with the words themselves. Over-apologizing often hides in plain sight, woven into everyday phrases that seem polite but quietly undermine you.

Listen for these subtle culprits:

· "Sorry, can I just ask a quick question?"

- "I'm sorry, but I think maybe..."
- "Sorry if this is a dumb idea."

Notice the common thread? Each one makes you smaller before you even share your thought. It's like walking into a room and immediately apologizing for taking up air.

Language habits form quickly because they're efficient. Your brain learns: *If I add sorry, people won't be mad. If I soften my request, maybe I'll be safer.* So the words become a script you run without thinking.

But once you start paying attention, you'll realize how often "sorry" sneaks into your language when it doesn't belong. And here's the good news: language habits are one of the easiest places to begin changing the reflex, because you can replace them with stronger, truer words. (We'll dive into swaps later, but for now, just noticing is powerful.)

Mini Exercise: Language Awareness

- Keep a sticky note by your desk or a notes app open on your phone.
- Every time you catch yourself writing or saying "sorry," jot down the phrase.
- At the end of the day, read them out loud. Ask yourself: Did this apology reflect real accountability—or was it a reflex?

Situational Triggers: Where Sorry Shows Up Most

Language is only half the story. The other half is context. Certain situations bring out the sorry reflex more than others.

Think about your day. Do you find yourself apologizing more often...

26

- **At work?** For asking questions, needing clarity, or setting boundaries?
- **With friends?** For being late, canceling plans, or not texting back quickly enough?
- **With strangers?** For taking up space in a crowded store, bumping someone's cart, or simply existing in their line of sight?
- **At home?** For needing rest, not keeping the house spotless, or being in a bad mood?

Each of us has different apology hotspots. For some, work meetings are the danger zone. For others, it's family gatherings. Spotting your triggers helps you anticipate when the reflex is most likely to surface—so you can practice interrupting it.

Case Story: Leah and the Grocery Store

Leah was shocked when she did a "sorry tally" one day. The majority weren't at work or with friends—they were at the grocery store. She said sorry when reaching for an item on the shelf, sorry when someone bumped her cart, sorry when she dropped a can. At the end of her shopping trip, she counted 19 apologies.

Once she noticed this, Leah realized her sorry reflex wasn't about actual mistakes—it was about existing in a space where she felt she was "in the way." Naming that pattern gave her power to experiment with other responses, like a polite "excuse me" or simply holding her ground with a smile.

Mini Exercise: Trigger Mapping

- For one week, track when and where you say sorry.
- Group them by setting: work, friends, family, strangers, home.

- Which context racks up the highest count? That's your starting place.

Body & Emotion Cues: The Physical Side of Sorry

Here's something most people miss: the sorry reflex doesn't start with words. It starts with your body.

Think about the last time you said sorry reflexively. Did you notice...

- A quick hunching of your shoulders?
- Nervous laughter?
- A tightening in your chest or stomach?

These physical cues often show up before the word. Your body registers a perceived threat, reacts with a small contraction, and the word "sorry" follows like a release valve.

Learning to recognize these cues is like spotting the first rumble of an earthquake. If you notice them early, you can pause before the full reflex takes over.

Case Story: Andre's Nervous Smile

Andre realized he apologized every time he laughed nervously. Someone would interrupt him at work, and before he could process his frustration, he'd smile, chuckle, and say "sorry." It wasn't that he felt guilty—it was that his body was uncomfortable with confrontation. The smile was his shield, and the apology was his escape route.

By noticing that smile as his early warning sign, Andre was able to catch himself mid-reflex. Instead of apologizing, he practiced taking a slow breath and continuing his sentence. Small change, big shift.

Mini Exercise: Body Scan

· The next time you catch yourself saying sorry, pause.
· Ask: What did my body feel in that moment?
· Was I shrinking, tightening, laughing, fidgeting?
· Keep a log of these cues. Over time, you'll notice patterns.

Why Patterns Matter

You might wonder: Why spend so much time noticing? Why not just force myself to stop saying sorry?

Because without awareness, change doesn't stick. Imagine trying to stop biting your nails without noticing when your hand goes to your mouth. You'd be fighting blind.

Spotting your patterns gives you a map. It shows you not only when and where the reflex shows up, but also *why*. And once you can see it, you can start to choose differently.

This chapter isn't about shaming yourself for the number of apologies you tally. It's about collecting data on your own habits with curiosity. Like a scientist studying a fascinating phenomenon—you're observing, recording, and gently asking: *What's really going on here?*

Closing Thought for Chapter 5

Your "sorry" has a story. It has words it clings to, situations it loves, and body cues it follows. The more you learn to spot those patterns, the more power you gain to pause, interrupt, and eventually replace them.

So grab your notebook, track your words, notice your triggers, and listen to your body. Each observation is a step closer to freedom.

In the next chapter, we'll go deeper into the difference between real apologies and reflexive ones—because not every sorry is bad. In fact, learning to tell the difference between genuine accountability and needless self-blame may be one of the most freeing shifts of all.

6

The Difference Between Real & Reflex Apologies

Not all apologies are created equal. Some are powerful acts of repair—bridges that reconnect us when harm has been done. Others are little more than nervous reflexes, words tossed out without substance. If you want to stop over-apologizing, the first step isn't to erase "sorry" from your vocabulary—it's to learn the difference between a real apology and a reflexive one.

This chapter will help you sort them out. We'll explore what makes a genuine apology meaningful, what reflexive apologies are missing, and why blurring the two can confuse both you and the people around you. By the end, you'll know when "sorry" is a tool of healing—and when it's just a habit dragging you down.

What a Real Apology Requires

A real apology is not complicated, but it is intentional. Think of it as a recipe with three ingredients:

1. **Ownership** — You take responsibility for the specific thing

you did or said. No excuses, no vague language.

2. **Acknowledgment** — You recognize the impact your action had on the other person. You see their feelings and validate them.

3. **Commitment** — You express a desire or plan to change, to avoid repeating the harm.

Here's an example:

"I'm sorry I interrupted you in the meeting. I realize that cut you off mid-thought and may have made you feel dismissed. I'll be more mindful to let you finish next time."

Notice the difference? It's clear, it's direct, and it centers the other person's experience—not the apologizer's guilt.

A real apology is an act of repair. It says: *I see you, I value you, and I want to make this right.* When given sincerely, it can actually strengthen relationships rather than weaken them.

What Reflexive Apologies Lack

Now let's contrast that with the reflexive apology.

"Sorry if I'm talking too much."

"Sorry, I probably don't make sense."

"Sorry, I just had a quick thought."

These aren't apologies at all. They don't name a real action or harm. They don't acknowledge impact. They don't commit to change. They're fillers—anxious attempts to soften your presence, shrink your needs, or preempt conflict that may not even exist.

Reflexive apologies have three big problems:

· **They blur meaning.** When "sorry" is sprinkled everywhere,

it loses weight. People stop recognizing when you're truly trying to repair harm.
- **They center you.** Instead of attending to someone else's experience, reflexive apologies focus on your fear of being a burden.
- **They create confusion.** Others may not know what you're apologizing for—or worse, they may assume you've done something wrong when you haven't.

Imagine texting a friend: "Sorry, I can't make dinner tonight." On the surface, it seems polite. But what are you really saying? Are you taking responsibility for breaking a promise? Or are you simply declining because life is busy? Reflexive apologies often muddy the waters, leaving everyone uncertain.

The Consequences of Blurred Boundaries

When you don't distinguish between real and reflexive apologies, boundaries get messy—for both you and the people around you.

- **For you:** You end up carrying guilt that doesn't belong to you. Every time you say sorry for existing, you reinforce the belief that your needs are wrong.
- **For others:** They may become unsure of when your apologies actually mean something. If you're always sorry, how do they know when you're truly accountable?

Over time, this can create a disconnect. The people in your life may stop trusting your words, not because you're dishonest, but because your language doesn't match reality. And you may begin to feel resentful—like no one takes your apologies seriously or like you're constantly walking on eggshells.

One client described it like this: "It's like I handed out a thousand discount coupons for free apologies. By the time I really needed to repair something, nobody valued them anymore."

Case Story: Priya's Friendships

Priya noticed she was the "sorry queen" in her friend group. If she had to cancel plans, she apologized. If she texted back late, she apologized. If she didn't laugh at a joke right away, she apologized.

Her friends started teasing her about it—"Don't worry, Priya, you don't have to be sorry for existing." At first, she laughed along. But inside, she felt embarrassed and frustrated. She *was* genuinely sorry when she hurt someone, but she realized her constant reflexive sorries had made her sincere ones harder to hear.

When Priya began practicing the difference—saving apologies for true missteps and replacing reflexive ones with clear, kind statements—her friendships shifted. Her friends felt less pressured, and she felt more authentic. And when she did need to say sorry, it landed. People trusted her words again.

Exercises: Sorting Real vs. Reflexive

To sharpen your awareness, try these exercises:
   1. The Apology Journal

- For one week, write down every apology you make.
- Next to each one, label it: *Real* or *Reflexive.*

34

- Ask: Did I take responsibility for something specific? Did I acknowledge someone else's experience? Did I commit to change?

2. The Reframe Test

- Take one reflexive apology you use often. For example: "Sorry I'm late."
- Ask: Was I truly at fault—or was this just life happening?
- Reframe: "Thanks for waiting for me." Notice how it shifts the dynamic.

3. Practice Saying Nothing

- When you feel the urge to say sorry but aren't sure why, try pausing instead. Let the silence hang for a moment. See what happens. Often, nothing bad at all.

Closing Thought for Chapter 6

Here's the truth: not all "sorrys" are bad. In fact, a real apology is one of the most powerful relational tools you'll ever have. But reflexive apologies? They're like static—cluttering your communication and clouding your self-worth.

Learning to tell the difference is like cleaning the lenses of your glasses. Suddenly, you can see clearly: when repair is needed, you step up with sincerity. When it isn't, you stop carrying false guilt.

In the next chapter, we'll dive into the words themselves— the language habits that sneak "sorry" into your sentences and how to replace them with stronger, clearer alternatives. Think of it as an apology detox for your vocabulary.

7

The Language Audit

Words are powerful. They shape how others see you, and more importantly, how you see yourself. Every reflexive "sorry" may feel small, but over time, those words create a script—a running commentary about your worth, your presence, and your right to take up space.

If you want to break the habit of over-apologizing, one of the most practical places to start is your vocabulary. In this chapter, we'll take a "language audit"—a close look at the words and phrases that sneak self-doubt into your communication—and we'll swap them for language that conveys confidence without sacrificing kindness.

Words That Signal Weakness

Certain words work like tiny leaks in your confidence. On their own, they don't look like much, but string enough of them together and your message loses its power. Let's look at the biggest culprits:

1. "Just"

- *"I just wanted to check in."*
- *"I'm just wondering if you have a minute."*
- *"I just thought maybe we could try this."*

That one little word makes your request sound smaller, less urgent, less valuable. It suggests you're apologizing for asking at all.

2. "I think" (when you already know)

- *"I think this might work."*
- *"I think we should consider..."*

Sometimes "I think" is appropriate—it signals opinion rather than fact. But often, it's a hedge. It's a way of softening your authority, as if you're afraid of being wrong.

3. "If that's okay"

- *"I'll send it by Thursday, if that's okay."*
- *"I'd like to add something, if that's okay."*

On the surface, it seems polite. But hidden inside is a request for permission to exist.

None of these words are evil on their own. But used reflexively, they create an apologetic tone that doesn't match your intention.

Neutralizing Fillers

The good news is that you don't have to overhaul your entire vocabulary—you just need to swap out a few common fillers. Think of it like cleaning out your closet. You don't need to throw everything away; you just need to replace what no longer fits.

Swap "sorry" with gratitude.

- Instead of: *"Sorry I'm late."*
- Try: *"Thank you for waiting."*

Swap "just" with directness.

- Instead of: *"I just wanted to check if you got my email."*
- Try: *"I wanted to check if you got my email."*

Swap "I think" with clarity.

- Instead of: *"I think we should go with option B."*
- Try: *"I recommend option B."*

Swap "if that's okay" with assurance.

- Instead of: *"I'll schedule it for Friday, if that's okay."*
- Try: *"I'll schedule it for Friday."*

These swaps may feel uncomfortable at first, like trying on shoes that are a little stiff. But the more you wear them, the more natural they'll feel—and the stronger your communication will sound.

Building a Confident Vocabulary

Language isn't just about avoiding weak words. It's also about actively building a vocabulary of strength, clarity, and kindness. Here's how:

1. Use declarative sentences.
Instead of hedging with questions, try stating clearly.

- "Can I maybe add something?" → "I'd like to add something."

2. Lead with clarity, not apology.
Start your emails and conversations with what you mean, not an apology.

- "Sorry for bothering you—do you have time to review this?" → "Do you have time to review this?"

3. Balance directness with warmth.
Confidence doesn't mean being cold. You can be both clear and kind.

- "I recommend option A because it's more efficient."
- Add warmth with: "I think it'll make your job easier, too."

When you practice these small shifts, you begin to hear yourself differently. You start believing that your ideas are worth sharing, your requests are valid, and your presence is welcome. And that belief changes how others respond to you.

Case Story: Emily's Emails

Emily worked in marketing and noticed her emails were packed with apologies. "Sorry to follow up," "Sorry for the delay," "Just checking in." She thought she was being polite, but her manager pulled her aside one day and said, "Emily, you don't need to apologize for doing your job."

At first, Emily felt embarrassed. But then she decided to try a little experiment. For one week, she swapped out "sorry" for gratitude or directness.

Instead of: *"Sorry for the delay—here's the file."*

She wrote: *"Thanks for your patience—here's the file."*

Instead of: *"Just checking in to see if you got my email."*

She wrote: *"I wanted to check if you got my email."*

Her colleagues didn't think she was rude. They thought she was confident. Emily realized that her language wasn't just communicating tasks—it was communicating her self-image. And once she shifted her words, her own sense of authority grew.

Exercises: Your Language Audit

Try these practices to sharpen your awareness and begin swapping weak words for strong ones:

1. The Email Clean-Up

- Before sending your next email, scan for "sorry," "just," "I think," or "if that's okay."
- Replace them with clearer alternatives.
- Hit send and notice how different it feels.

2. The Mirror Test

- Say a reflexive phrase out loud (e.g., "Sorry, I just wanted to add something").
- Then say the confident version ("I'd like to add something").

- Look at your face and posture as you say each one. Which version feels more aligned with how you want to show up?

3. Build a Swap List

- Create a running list of your common weak phrases and their replacements.
- Keep it handy until the new language becomes second nature.

Closing Thought for Chapter 7

Words are not just words. They're stories you tell about yourself—tiny scripts that either shrink you or strengthen you. When you shift from reflexive, apologetic language to clear, confident words, you change not only how others see you, but how you see yourself.

You don't need to bulldoze. You don't need to strip kindness from your speech. You simply need to remove the apology filter that's been dulling your voice.

In the next chapter, we'll dive deeper into one of the biggest areas where apologies show up: boundaries. Because language isn't just about words—it's about knowing where you end and others begin. And if "sorry" has been your shield, boundaries are the next skill you'll need to practice.

8

Boundaries & Sorry

If "sorry" is your shield, boundaries are the thing you've been protecting all along. Many people who over-apologize do so because boundaries feel uncomfortable, even unsafe. Saying no feels like rejection. Asking for space feels selfish. Asserting needs feels like conflict.

So what do we do instead? We apologize. We smooth things over. We hope that if we can keep everyone happy, we won't have to deal with the messy business of setting limits.

But here's the truth: healthy boundaries and confident communication go hand in hand. Learning to say no without apology isn't about becoming rude or selfish—it's about learning to live from a place of honesty rather than guilt.

Why Boundaries Feel Like Conflict

If you struggle with boundaries, you're not broken—you've likely been conditioned to believe that saying no equals being difficult. For many, this lesson starts early.

- Maybe you were praised for being the "easy child" who never asked for much.
- Maybe you were punished or shamed for pushing back, so you learned to stay quiet.
- Maybe your culture or family taught you that your role was to accommodate others, even at the expense of yourself.

These lessons stick. By adulthood, saying no doesn't just feel uncomfortable—it feels dangerous. Your nervous system interprets it as conflict, and conflict feels like a threat. Cue the fawn response. Cue the "sorry."

Instead of: *"No, I can't take that on."*

You say: *"Sorry, I'll try to make it work."*

Instead of: *"I need some quiet time tonight."*

You say: *"Sorry, maybe another time."*

Instead of honoring your needs, you use apology to soften them, hoping it will protect you from backlash.

Saying No Without Sorry

Here's the good news: boundaries can be expressed with clarity and kindness, no apology required. You can decline without guilt, set limits without anger, and honor yourself without abandoning others.

Here are a few examples:

- **Declining an invitation:**
- Reflexive: *"Sorry, I can't make it."*
- Confident: *"Thanks for inviting me, but I won't be able to come."*
- **Turning down extra work:**

44

- Reflexive: *"Sorry, I don't think I can take this on."*
- Confident: *"I don't have capacity for this right now. Let's revisit priorities."*
- **Needing time alone:**
- Reflexive: *"Sorry, I just need a little space."*
- Confident: *"I'm going to take some time for myself tonight, but let's catch up later."*

Notice the difference. The confident versions are still kind. They acknowledge the other person. But they also stand firmly in your truth, without dragging guilt into the room.

The first few times you try this, your body may rebel. Your heart may race. Your brain may scream: *They'll hate me! They'll leave me! I'm being selfish!* That's normal. Remember: your nervous system has been trained for years to equate boundaries with danger. But practice rewires that response.

Rebuilding Trust With Yourself

Every time you set a boundary without apology, you're sending yourself a message: *I can handle this. My needs matter. I trust myself to stand my ground.*

This is important, because many people who over-apologize don't trust themselves in conflict. They fear that if they push back, they'll either explode in anger or collapse in guilt. So they default to apology as the safer route.

Boundaries help rebuild that inner trust. They show you that you can survive saying no—that you can speak clearly without losing relationships, and that your needs aren't a burden but a natural part of being human.

One client described her journey like this: "The first time I said no to a family obligation without apologizing, I thought I might throw up. But when nothing terrible happened—when my family still loved me, when the world kept turning—I realized: maybe I'm not the villain after all. Maybe I'm just a person with limits."

Case Story: Marcus and the Office Hours

Marcus was a high school teacher who loved his students. But he also loved his evenings with his family. The problem? He found himself apologizing constantly for enforcing his office hours.

"Sorry, I can't stay late today."

"Sorry, you'll have to email me instead."

"Sorry, I know you wanted extra help."

He meant well—he didn't want students to feel brushed off. But the more he apologized, the more his boundaries eroded. Students began expecting he'd be available at all times. His evenings disappeared. His frustration grew.

One day, Marcus decided to try a new approach. Instead of apologizing, he simply stated: "I'm available until 3:30. After that, I'll respond to emails tomorrow." He said it kindly but clearly. No apology attached.

To his surprise, students respected it. They didn't storm out. They didn't hate him. They adjusted. And Marcus went home on time, guilt-free.

Exercises: Practicing Boundaries Without Sorry

1. The Boundary Script

Write out a boundary you've been struggling to set. For example: "I can't take on extra work right now."

- Reflexive version: Add your usual apology.
- Confident version: Rewrite it without "sorry."
- Practice saying both out loud. Notice how they feel different in your body.

2. The Small No

Choose one small situation this week where you can practice saying no without apology. Maybe it's declining a coffee invitation, or not answering emails after hours. Start small, build confidence.

3. The Aftermath Reflection

After you set a boundary, write down what actually happened. Did the other person explode—or did they accept it? Did your worst fear come true—or was it easier than expected? Documenting reality helps retrain your nervous system.

Closing Thought for Chapter 8

Boundaries and apologies are not enemies—but they do need to be separated. Boundaries say: *This is who I am, this is what I can offer, and this is what I can't.* Apologies say: *I recognize I've caused harm and want to repair it.* When you mix the two, you water down both.

Learning to set boundaries without sorry isn't selfish. It's honest. It's respectful—to yourself and to others. Because when you show up with clarity instead of guilt, people know exactly where you stand. And that's not rejection—it's connection.

In the next chapter, we'll look at the subtle ways "sorry" disguises itself—not as kindness, but as avoidance. Because sometimes, apologizing isn't about peace at all. It's about hiding what we really feel.

9

When Sorry Is a Mask

Sometimes "sorry" isn't really about politeness—or even fear. Sometimes it's a disguise. It's the mask we wear when we're uncomfortable being honest about what we feel or need. We use apology to cover up emotions we don't know how to express, or to sidestep conversations that feel too risky.

On the surface, this looks like humility. Underneath, it's avoidance. And the longer you wear that mask, the harder it is to show up authentically in your relationships.

This chapter will help you uncover the times when "sorry" isn't about repair or reflex—it's about hiding.

Sorry as Avoidance

Apologies can be a way of dodging uncomfortable emotions. Anger, disappointment, frustration, even sadness—these feelings can feel dangerous to express, especially if you grew up in an environment where big emotions weren't welcomed.

So instead of saying, *"I'm upset you didn't follow through,"* you say, *"Sorry, I shouldn't have expected so much."*

Instead of saying, *"I'm hurt that you canceled on me again,"* you say, *"Sorry, I know you're busy."*

Notice what happened? The real feeling—anger, hurt, disappointment—gets swallowed. The apology acts like a lid, sealing it in. The relationship looks smoother on the outside, but inside, resentment brews.

Avoidance apologies may protect you from conflict in the short term, but they cost you intimacy in the long term. You can't build true closeness if you're always apologizing for having needs.

Sorry as Permission-Seeking

Sometimes "sorry" isn't about avoidance—it's about asking for permission to exist. It's a way of saying, *"Am I okay? Do you still accept me? Will you let me take up this space?"*

Think about phrases like:

- *"Sorry, can I ask a dumb question?"*
- *"Sorry, I need to run to the restroom."*
- *"Sorry, could you help me with this?"*

None of these things require an apology. Questions aren't dumb, bathrooms are human, and asking for help is normal. But when you attach "sorry," you're really saying: *Please don't be mad at me for needing this.*

This is what happens when your self-worth hinges on others' approval. The apology is a test: *Will you still like me even if I'm inconvenient?*

The irony is that most people don't even notice the "inconvenience." They only hear your apology and wonder why you're apologizing for being human.

Sorry as Self-Eraser

The most painful form of mask–apology is the one that erases your needs entirely. This shows up when you minimize yourself to make others more comfortable.

- You apologize for expressing joy, as if being too happy might bother someone.
- You apologize for speaking passionately about something you care about, as if your enthusiasm takes up too much air.
- You apologize for having boundaries, as if needing rest or space is a flaw.

Over time, this form of apology eats away at your sense of identity. You become the person who's always sorry, always agreeable, always invisible. And invisibility feels safe—but it's also lonely.

Case Story: Nina's Marriage

Nina was in her forties, married for over a decade, with two kids and a busy life. She noticed that in her marriage, "sorry" had become her default word.

When her husband forgot their anniversary, she said, *"Sorry, I shouldn't have made a big deal about it."*

When he was late picking up the kids, she said, *"Sorry, I should've reminded you earlier."*

When she felt lonely, she said, *"Sorry, I know you're tired."*

In each case, Nina was covering her true feelings—hurt,

disappointment, desire for connection—with apologies. On the outside, she looked like the peacemaker. On the inside, she felt invisible.

When she finally stopped apologizing and began naming her feelings, something shifted. It wasn't easy. There were awkward conversations, tense silences, moments of fear. But there was also honesty. Her husband began to see her more clearly. Their marriage became less about smoothing over conflict and more about facing it together.

Nina realized her apologies hadn't been protecting her marriage—they'd been suffocating it.

Exercises: Spotting the Mask

1. The Emotion Swap

- The next time you apologize, ask yourself: *What emotion am I covering up?*
- Write down the apology you said, then rewrite it with the real emotion.
- Example: "Sorry I'm so emotional." → "I feel sad and need support."

2. Permission Check

- Notice when you apologize for basic needs (asking a question, using the restroom, needing help).
- Pause and remind yourself: *This is human, not a crime.*
- Try stating the need without apology: "I need a quick break."

3. Visibility Challenge

- Choose one place where you tend to shrink—maybe a meeting, a friendship, or at home.
- For one week, experiment with removing apologies that minimize your presence.
- Instead of apologizing for speaking, state your point. Instead of apologizing for joy, let yourself shine.

Closing Thought for Chapter 9

Sometimes "sorry" is honest. Sometimes it's reflex. And sometimes, it's a mask. Recognizing when you're using apology to cover feelings, seek permission, or erase yourself is the first step to taking the mask off.

When you stop apologizing for your emotions, your needs, and your humanity, you create space for something far more powerful: authenticity. The people who love you don't want the masked version of you—they want the real you.

In the next chapter, we'll explore how to reframe conflict itself—not as something to be feared or smoothed over, but as an opportunity for deeper connection. Because when you stop hiding behind "sorry," you start discovering what honesty can really do.

10

Reframing Conflict

For many people who over-apologize, conflict feels like the ultimate danger zone. You'll do almost anything to avoid it—smooth things over, swallow your feelings, apologize for things that aren't your fault—just to keep the peace.

But what if conflict wasn't something to fear? What if, instead of being the enemy, conflict could actually be the doorway to deeper trust, stronger relationships, and more authentic connection?

This chapter is about rethinking conflict—not as something to avoid at all costs, but as something you can step into with clarity, courage, and even curiosity.

Conflict as Growth, Not Danger

Our nervous systems are wired to see conflict as a threat. Raised voices, tense silence, even subtle disagreements can make your heart race and your stomach churn. For people with a strong "sorry reflex," the instinct is immediate: apologize, appease, fix.

But here's the truth: conflict is simply two truths colliding. It's not proof that the relationship is broken. It's proof that two human beings are showing up with different perspectives, needs, or experiences.

Healthy conflict can actually strengthen relationships. When handled well, it creates:

- **Clarity:** You understand each other better.
- **Trust:** You prove you can survive disagreement without leaving each other.
- **Growth:** You learn how to show up more authentically, without hiding behind apologies.

Think about your closest relationships. Chances are, they haven't been built on perfect harmony. They've been built on moments of friction that led to deeper understanding.

De-Shaming Disagreement

One reason conflict feels so terrifying is because we attach shame to it. We believe:

- If I disagree, I'm being difficult.
- If I push back, I'll lose love.
- If I cause conflict, I'm a bad person.

But disagreement is not disrespect. Boundaries are not rejection. Expressing your truth is not cruelty.

When you de-shame conflict, you give yourself permission to show up fully without needing to apologize for every ripple you cause.

Here's a reframing exercise:

· Instead of: *"I'm sorry I disagreed with you."*
· Try: *"I see this differently, and I'd like to talk it through."*

The first response centers shame. The second centers honesty. Which one creates space for a real relationship?

Building Conflict Resilience

Of course, shifting how you see conflict doesn't happen overnight. Your nervous system may still light up, your hands may shake, and your brain may scream: *Run!* That's normal. Conflict resilience is something you build with practice.

Here are a few small steps:

1. Practice with low-stakes conflicts.

Start with situations that don't carry huge emotional weight—like telling a friend you'd rather see a different movie, or asking your partner to take the trash out when they forget. These small moments teach your body that disagreement doesn't equal disaster.

2. Use "I" statements.

Instead of blaming, focus on your experience.

· "You never listen to me" → "I feel unheard when I get interrupted."

3. Breathe before you respond.

Give your nervous system a chance to settle before you speak. A pause of even three seconds can shift your tone from defensive to calm.

4. Resist the reflex apology.

When you feel "sorry" rising to your lips, pause. Ask: *Am I apologizing for harm—or for existing?* If it's the latter, try holding your ground instead.

Case Story: Jordan and the Roommate

Jordan shared an apartment with a close friend. For months, he apologized constantly for things that weren't his fault—like when the dishes piled up, or when his roommate left laundry in the dryer. "Sorry, I should've reminded you."

But the truth? Jordan wasn't at fault. He was using "sorry" as a way to avoid conflict. He feared that if he pointed out the imbalance, the friendship would suffer.

Finally, he reached a breaking point. Instead of apologizing, he said, "I feel frustrated when the dishes aren't done, because I end up doing more than my share. Can we figure out a system that works better?"

His roommate was surprised—but also relieved. He hadn't realized how much Jordan was holding in. They created a simple schedule, and the tension eased. Jordan realized conflict hadn't destroyed their friendship. It had saved it.

Exercises: Reframing Conflict

1. Conflict Reframe Journal

- Write down a recent conflict you avoided with an apology.
- Rewrite the scene as if you expressed your true feeling without sorry.
- Example: Instead of "Sorry I'm being difficult," try "I feel

strongly about this, and here's why."

2. Practice the Pause

- The next time you feel the urge to apologize in a disagreement, pause.
- Take three slow breaths.
- Ask: Is this apology repairing harm, or avoiding discomfort?

3. Low-Stakes Disagreements

- Intentionally practice disagreeing in small ways this week.
- Say, "I'd rather eat at X restaurant," or "I actually liked the other idea better."
- Notice how people respond. Most often, they accept it without issue—and you build resilience.

Closing Thought for Chapter 10

Conflict is not the monster under the bed. It's not proof that you're unlovable or wrong. It's a natural part of being human. And when you stop apologizing for every disagreement, you open the door to relationships that are more honest, more resilient, and more real.

You don't need to erase conflict—you need to reframe it. Instead of running from it, you can step into it with clarity and courage.

In the next chapter, we'll explore one of the most powerful language swaps you can make: turning "sorry" into "thank you." Because sometimes, the simplest change in words transforms the entire dynamic of a relationship.

11

From Sorry to Thank You

What if I told you that the fastest way to stop over-apologizing isn't to cut "sorry" out of your vocabulary—but to swap it for two simple words: *thank you*?

This may sound almost too easy, but it's one of the most powerful shifts you can make. Where "sorry" drags you down into guilt and self-blame, "thank you" lifts the interaction up into gratitude and connection. One diminishes you; the other affirms both you and the other person.

In this chapter, we'll explore why this small swap works so well, how to practice it in everyday life, and what it can do to reshape not just your words, but your relationships.

Gratitude Swap: The Power of Reframing

Think about the difference between these two phrases:

- *"Sorry I'm late."*
- *"Thank you for waiting."*

The first centers your guilt. It frames the interaction as a failure on your part. The second centers the other person's kindness. It shifts the energy away from shame and into appreciation.

Or take this example:

- *"Sorry I'm being emotional."*
- *"Thank you for listening to me while I share this."*

One suggests you're a burden. The other highlights the gift of being heard.

By reframing apologies into gratitude, you don't deny what happened—you simply choose to spotlight what strengthens connection rather than what erodes it.

Why this works:

1. Gratitude builds trust. It makes people feel valued rather than inconvenienced.
2. Gratitude strengthens relationships. It highlights care instead of fault.
3. Gratitude rewires your own brain. Over time, you start to see situations not through the lens of guilt, but through the lens of appreciation.

Appreciation as Assertiveness

Many people believe that confidence means being blunt or cold. But gratitude shows another way: you can be warm and kind while also being clear and unapologetic.

For example:

- Instead of: *"Sorry to bother you with another question."*

- Try: *"Thank you for taking the time to clarify this for me."*
- Instead of: *"Sorry I can't make it tonight."*
- Try: *"Thank you for understanding that I need to rest."*

Notice how these phrases not only remove guilt—they actually strengthen the bond. The other person feels appreciated, and you feel more grounded in your choice.

Appreciation is assertive because it says: *I belong here. My needs are valid. I trust that you can handle this.* And when you speak from that place, you invite mutual respect rather than one-sided guilt.

Practical Swaps: Everyday Scenarios

Let's put this into practice with a few common examples:

- **At Work**
- Reflex: *"Sorry this took me so long."*
- Swap: *"Thank you for your patience while I got this right."*
- **With Friends**
- Reflex: *"Sorry I've been so hard to reach lately."*
- Swap: *"Thank you for being patient while I've had a lot on my plate."*
- **In Relationships**
- Reflex: *"Sorry I need some time to myself."*
- Swap: *"Thank you for giving me space to recharge."*
- **With Strangers**
- Reflex: *"Sorry for bumping into you."* (when it wasn't even your fault)
- Swap: *"Thanks for moving over."*

You're not ignoring what happened. You're simply framing it in a way that strengthens connection instead of shrinking you.

Case Story 1: Melissa and the Meeting

Melissa, a mid-level manager, realized she began almost every presentation with: *"Sorry if this is boring."* or *"Sorry if I go on too long."*

Her mentor pointed out how undermining this was. Together, they tried a gratitude swap. At her next meeting, instead of apologizing, she began with: *"Thank you for taking the time to hear this update. I know your schedule is full, and I appreciate your focus."*

The difference was immediate. Her team leaned in. They felt valued rather than burdened. And Melissa felt her own confidence rise just by changing those words.

Case Story 2: Omar and His Partner

Omar had a habit of apologizing every time he expressed stress at home. If he vented about work, he'd say: *"Sorry, I don't mean to dump this on you."* If he got emotional, he'd say: *"Sorry, I know this is too much."*

His partner reassured him repeatedly that it was okay, but Omar still felt guilty. One evening, he decided to try a swap. Instead of saying sorry, he said: *"Thank you for listening—I really needed to get that off my chest."*

His partner's eyes softened. "I like when you let me in," she said. "It makes me feel closer to you."

That was the moment Omar realized: his apologies had been creating distance. Gratitude created connection.

Case Story 3: Alina and Her Kids

Alina was a single mom who apologized constantly to her children: *"Sorry we can't afford that toy." "Sorry I can't pick you up earlier." "Sorry dinner is late."*

She noticed how heavy her kids began to feel—as though they were the reason she was always guilty.

One day, she swapped the script. Instead of apologizing, she started saying: *"Thank you for being patient." "Thank you for understanding that we can't buy everything we want right now." "Thank you for helping me out while dinner was running late."*

Her kids lit up. They felt proud instead of burdensome. And Alina felt lighter, too. She realized that gratitude didn't just change her words—it changed the energy of her home.

Exercises: Practicing the Swap

1. The Gratitude Journal Swap

- Each day, write down three moments when you apologized.
- Rewrite each as a gratitude statement.
- Example: "Sorry I missed your call" → "Thank you for reaching out—I'll call you back now."

2. The Out-Loud Practice

- Choose a common reflex apology you use (like "Sorry I'm late").
- Stand in front of a mirror and practice saying both the reflex and the gratitude swap.
- Notice the difference in your posture, tone, and how you

feel inside.

3. The Family/Friend Experiment

- Tell one trusted person you're practicing this swap.
- Ask them to notice when you say "thank you" instead of "sorry."
- After a week, ask them how it felt to hear gratitude instead of apology.

The Ripple Effect of Gratitude

Here's the beautiful part: swapping sorry for thank you doesn't just change *you*. It changes your relationships.

When you apologize reflexively, the other person is put in the role of comforter. They have to wave it off, reassure you, or dismiss the guilt. But when you thank them, you put them in the role of contributor. They feel appreciated, valued, and seen.

Over time, this creates a ripple effect:

- People trust you more, because your words feel intentional.
- People enjoy being around you more, because gratitude is contagious.
- You enjoy being around yourself more, because you're no longer carrying the weight of unnecessary guilt.

Closing Thought for Chapter 11

Replacing "sorry" with "thank you" may be the simplest tool in this book, but it's also one of the most transformative. It shifts energy from guilt to gratitude, from self-erasure to mutual respect.

Every time you say "thank you" instead of "sorry," you're telling yourself: *My presence isn't a burden. My needs aren't shameful. My relationships don't need guilt to survive—they thrive on appreciation.*

In the next chapter, we'll build on this momentum by rewriting your everyday scripts. From emails to conversations, you'll learn how to craft language that reflects your true confidence, so that "thank you" becomes the beginning of a whole new way of speaking.

12

Rewriting Scripts

By now, you've started spotting your "sorry reflex," practicing gratitude swaps, and experimenting with healthier boundaries. But let's face it—habits this ingrained don't vanish overnight. If "sorry" has been stitched into your everyday communication, you'll need a toolkit of ready-made replacements.

That's what this chapter is about: rewriting your scripts. From emails to work meetings, from family conversations to texts with friends, you'll learn how to replace reflexive apologies with words that feel confident, kind, and true.

Think of this as your language renovation project. We're not tearing the whole house down. We're updating the places that squeak, leak, and sag—so your words support you instead of undermining you.

Everyday Situations: From Reflex to Rewrite

Let's start with the most common places where unnecessary apologies sneak in.

1. Email Openers

- Reflex: *"Sorry to bother you, but..."*
- Rewrite: *"I wanted to follow up on..."*
- Reflex: *"Sorry for the delay."*
- Rewrite: *"Thank you for your patience."*

2. Work Meetings

- Reflex: *"Sorry, can I just add something?"*
- Rewrite: *"I'd like to add something."*
- Reflex: *"Sorry if this doesn't make sense."*
- Rewrite: *"Here's my thought—tell me what you think."*

3. Social Interactions

- Reflex: *"Sorry I can't come tonight."*
- Rewrite: *"Thanks for inviting me—I won't be able to make it, but I hope it's a great time."*
- Reflex: *"Sorry I'm such a mess."*
- Rewrite: *"Thanks for being patient with me while I figure this out."*

4. Family Conversations

- Reflex: *"Sorry I need some alone time."*
- Rewrite: *"I'm going to take some quiet time to recharge. I'll be back later."*

These rewrites may feel stiff at first, like breaking in new shoes. That's normal. With repetition, they'll start to feel natural—and you'll begin to notice how people respond differently when you speak from clarity rather than apology.

Direct Yet Warm: Finding the Middle Ground

One of the biggest fears about removing "sorry" is sounding harsh. You might worry: *If I stop apologizing, won't I seem rude? Won't people think I'm cold?*

Not at all. Confidence and kindness are not opposites. You can be clear without being cutting. You can be warm without being weak. The key is balance.

Tips for warm confidence:

- **Use gratitude:** "Thanks for sharing that with me" softens a disagreement without apology.
- **Add curiosity:** "Tell me more about how you see it" invites dialogue without self-erasure.
- **Mirror empathy:** "I hear that this was frustrating for you" shows care without slipping into guilt.

Think of your words like music. Too many apologies turn down the volume of your voice. Removing every soft note can make the song too sharp. But balance—clarity with warmth—creates harmony.

Case Story 1: Devon's Weekly Report

Devon was a junior analyst who dreaded sending his weekly reports. Every email began with: *"Sorry this is so long."* or *"Sorry if this is confusing."*

When his manager suggested he cut the apologies, Devon panicked. "Won't they think I'm arrogant?" he asked.

Instead, Devon tried a rewrite: *"Here's this week's report. I've highlighted the key findings and included supporting details below."*

The difference was night and day. His colleagues didn't find him arrogant—they found him clear. And Devon discovered something important: clarity is respectful. Apologies weren't making him polite. They were making him harder to understand.

Case Story 2: Tasha and Her Best Friend

Tasha's best friend often invited her to social events, but Tasha, an introvert, couldn't always go. Every time she declined, she said: *"Sorry, I'm the worst. Sorry I can't be there. Sorry, sorry, sorry."*

Her friend finally laughed and said, "You don't need to keep apologizing—I just want to know if you can come or not!"

Tasha experimented with a rewrite: *"Thanks for inviting me! I can't make it tonight, but I hope you have the best time."*

Her friend didn't feel rejected. She felt appreciated. Tasha realized the friendship didn't need endless apologies—it needed honesty and gratitude.

Case Story 3: Ramon and His Kids

Ramon, a single dad, noticed he apologized to his kids constantly: *"Sorry, I burned dinner." "Sorry, I forgot your homework." "Sorry, I'm so stressed."*

He worried his kids were starting to see him as unreliable. So he rewrote his scripts. Instead of "sorry," he tried: *"Thanks for being patient while I fix dinner." "Thanks for reminding me about your homework—I'll help now."*

To his surprise, his kids started responding differently. They smiled more, pitched in more, and seemed proud to be part of the solution. Ramon realized: his kids didn't need his guilt—they needed his leadership.

Roleplay Practice: Learning in Safe Spaces

One of the best ways to practice new scripts is roleplay. It may feel silly, but practicing in low-stakes settings helps you find your voice when the real moment comes.

Here's how:

1. Ask a trusted friend, partner, or coach to roleplay common scenarios (like declining an invitation or asking for clarity at work).
2. Say your reflex apology first, just to notice how it feels.
3. Then say the rewritten confident version.
4. Reflect together: How did each land? What body language shifted?

This simple exercise builds muscle memory. The more you practice the confident version, the easier it becomes to reach for it in real life.

Exercises: Script Rewrite Toolkit

1. The Email Rewrite Challenge

- Pull up your sent emails from the past week.
- Highlight every "sorry," "just," or "if that's okay."
- Rewrite each sentence as if you could send it again with confidence.

2. Conversation Rehearsal

· Think of one upcoming situation where you're likely to apologize (asking your boss for clarification, telling your partner you need space, declining an invite).
· Write your reflex apology. Then write your confident rewrite.
· Practice saying it out loud three times before the actual conversation.

3. The Confident Script Bank

· Start a running list of rewritten phrases that feel authentic to you.
· Keep them on your phone or a sticky note until they become second nature.
· Example entries: "Thanks for waiting," "I'd like to add something," "I don't have capacity for that right now."

The Deeper Payoff: Identity Shift

At first, rewriting scripts may feel like surface-level wordplay. But the deeper you practice, the more profound the change.

Here's why: language shapes identity. When you stop apologizing reflexively, you start to see yourself differently. You stop seeing yourself as a burden and start seeing yourself as a participant. You stop feeling like an inconvenience and start feeling like an equal.

One client described it like this: "I thought I was just changing words. But after a few weeks, I noticed I stood taller in meetings. I looked people in the eye more. I even asked for a raise.

Changing my language changed me."

That's the power of rewriting scripts. It's not about memorizing stock phrases—it's about retraining your brain to believe: *I belong here. My words matter. My needs are valid.*

Closing Thought for Chapter 12

Rewriting your scripts isn't about sounding perfect. It's about sounding true. Every time you replace a reflexive "sorry" with clear, confident language, you rewire not just your communication but your self-concept.

So practice. Write them down. Roleplay them. Try them on. Make mistakes and try again. Over time, these new words will stop feeling forced and start feeling like your voice—the voice that was always there, hidden under layers of unnecessary apology.

In the next chapter, we'll turn inward and look at the body itself—because changing your words is powerful, but changing how your nervous system responds is just as important. You'll learn how to reset your system so that confidence doesn't just come from your mouth, but from the inside out.

13

Nervous System Reset

Up until now, we've talked a lot about words. Rewriting scripts. Swapping "sorry" for "thank you." Learning to speak without apology. But here's the truth: if your body is still in panic mode every time you assert yourself, the words won't stick.

That's because over-apologizing isn't only a language habit—it's a nervous system habit. Long before the word "sorry" leaves your lips, your body feels the rush: tight chest, shallow breath, racing heart, shoulders curling in. Your system interprets disagreement, disappointment, or even silence as danger. And your brain reaches for the fastest escape hatch: apology.

To change the reflex, you can't just change your vocabulary. You have to teach your body a new way to respond. This chapter will give you tools to reset your nervous system so you can stay steady, calm, and present—even in the moments that used to trigger your automatic "sorry."

Understanding the Triggers

Think of your nervous system like an alarm system. It's scanning constantly: *Am I safe? Am I accepted? Am I okay?* For someone prone to over-apologizing, that alarm is extra sensitive.

Triggers might include:

- A colleague sighing when you speak.
- A partner going quiet in an argument.
- A stranger brushing past you with a sharp look.
- Even just imagining you might have upset someone.

Your body reacts before your rational mind catches up. You feel heat in your face, a tightening in your throat, or an urge to shrink. That's your nervous system sounding the alarm.

Step one to resetting is awareness. Start noticing your body's cues: Where do you feel tension? What sensations come right before you blurt out "sorry"? Recognizing those signals is like spotting the smoke before the fire.

Calming Techniques for the Body

Once you notice the triggers, you need tools to soothe your system in the moment. Think of these as first-aid kits for your body when the alarm goes off.

1. Breathwork Reset

- Inhale slowly through your nose for a count of 4.
- Hold for a count of 2.
- Exhale through your mouth for a count of 6.

· This tells your body: *I'm safe. I can slow down.*

2. Grounding Through the Senses

When anxiety spikes, anchor yourself in the present:

· Name 5 things you can see.
· Name 4 things you can touch.
· Name 3 things you can hear.
· Name 2 things you can smell.
· Name 1 thing you can taste.
· This grounds you in reality, pulling you out of the spiral of "what ifs."

3. The Shoulder Drop

Notice if your shoulders are hunched by your ears. Drop them deliberately. Roll them back. Open your chest. This posture shift signals to your body that you're safe enough to expand, not shrink.

Building Tolerance for Discomfort

Resetting your nervous system isn't just about calming—it's about building resilience. You want your body to learn: *I can feel discomfort without needing to escape through apology.*

Here are a few ways to practice:

1. The Micro Pause

When you feel the urge to say sorry, pause for just two seconds. Let the silence hang. This tiny gap teaches your nervous system that discomfort won't kill you.

2. Gradual Exposure

Start with small challenges. Let yourself be a few minutes late to a casual meeting without apologizing. Ask a "dumb" question in class or at work. Each time you survive without apology, your body learns: *See? Nothing bad happened.*

3. Self-Compassion Mantras

When anxiety rises, repeat to yourself:

- "I am allowed to take up space."
- "Needing clarity is not a crime."
- "I can handle this moment without apologizing."
- Speaking kindness to your nervous system helps soothe its alarm.

Case Story 1: Claire at the Conference

Claire was giving a presentation at a professional conference. Public speaking terrified her. Her default strategy was to apologize at the start: *"Sorry if I ramble. Sorry if this isn't helpful."*

But she had been practicing nervous system resets. Before walking on stage, she took three slow breaths, planted her feet firmly on the ground, and repeated: *"I am allowed to be here."*

When she stepped up, her hands still shook—but she resisted the apology. Instead, she opened with: *"Thank you for being here today. I'm excited to share what I've learned."*

The audience leaned in. Claire felt her body steady. For the first time, she realized: confidence isn't about not feeling nervous—it's about knowing how to regulate your body when nerves hit.

Case Story 2: Luis and the Silent Boss

Luis dreaded his weekly check-ins. His boss was quiet, often frowning as she reviewed notes. Luis's body interpreted the silence as anger. His heart raced, and out popped: *"Sorry, I'll do better next time."*

But after learning grounding techniques, Luis tried something new. When the silence came, he pressed his feet into the floor and took one slow breath. He resisted the urge to fill the space with apology.

Finally, his boss looked up and said, "This report is solid. Let's move to the next one."

Luis realized he had been apologizing not for mistakes, but for silence. His nervous system was reacting to imagined danger. By pausing, he gave himself space to see the reality: his boss wasn't angry—just thoughtful.

Case Story 3: Maya and the Dinner Party

Maya often over-apologized in social settings. If she laughed too loudly, bumped a chair, or told a long story, she'd immediately say sorry.

One night at a dinner party, she decided to practice a new strategy. Every time she felt the urge to apologize, she paused and took a sip of water instead. She grounded herself in the clinking glasses, the hum of conversation, the warmth of the food.

By the end of the night, she hadn't said sorry once. Her friends didn't seem annoyed by her presence. In fact, they complimented her story. Maya realized that the only person who thought she was "too much" was her nervous system.

Exercises: Training Your Nervous System

1. Daily Regulation Practice

Spend five minutes each morning practicing a calming technique—breathwork, grounding, or gentle stretching. This builds a baseline of calm that makes you less reactive throughout the day.

2. The Sorry Pause Drill

Choose one situation this week where you know you'll be tempted to say sorry. Commit to pausing for two seconds before speaking. Use that pause to breathe, plant your feet, or drop your shoulders.

3. Comfort Zone Stretching

Pick one small discomfort to lean into each day: ask a stranger for directions, request help at work, or share your opinion in a group. Do it without apologizing. Afterwards, reflect: What did I fear? What actually happened?

The Science Behind It

When you practice calming and exposure, you're actually rewiring your brain. You're teaching your amygdala (the part of the brain that scans for danger) that not every sigh, silence, or disagreement equals threat.

Over time, the neural pathways that trigger "sorry" grow weaker. New pathways—ones that connect confidence with safety—grow stronger. This isn't just theory. Studies in neuroplasticity show that repeated small practices literally reshape the brain's response to stress.

So every pause, every breath, every moment you resist the reflex apology—it's not wasted. It's practice. It's your brain and body learning a new way of being.

Closing Thought for Chapter 13

Changing your words is powerful. But changing your nervous system is transformative. When your body learns that conflict, silence, or discomfort aren't threats, you stop needing apology as a shield.

Confidence isn't about never feeling fear. It's about knowing how to stay grounded when fear comes. Every breath, every pause, every moment of choosing gratitude instead of guilt—it all adds up.

In the next chapter, we'll look at one of the most visible arenas for this transformation: the workplace. Because if you can learn to speak without apology in professional settings—emails, meetings, interviews—you'll discover just how much authority and respect you've been giving away. And you'll learn how to take it back.

14

Workplace Confidence

Work is one of the biggest arenas where the "sorry reflex" shows up. Whether it's in emails, meetings, or performance reviews, many people default to apology as a way of softening themselves, smoothing conflict, or preemptively avoiding criticism.

On the surface, it looks like humility. But in reality, these apologies can undermine your authority, dilute your message, and even affect your career trajectory. If you want to build professional confidence, learning to speak and write without unnecessary apology is a non-negotiable skill.

This chapter will give you practical tools for transforming the way you show up at work—so your colleagues, clients, and bosses see you as competent, trustworthy, and confident (and so *you* begin to believe it, too).

Professional Scripts: Speaking Without Shrinking

Let's start with everyday work scenarios. Here are some common reflexive apologies, along with rewrites that project professionalism and confidence:

1. Asking for Clarification

- Reflex: *"Sorry, I'm not sure I understand. Could you explain again?"*
- Rewrite: *"I want to make sure I'm clear—could you explain that again?"*

2. Following Up

- Reflex: *"Sorry to bother you, just checking if you saw my email."*
- Rewrite: *"I'm following up on my earlier email. Do you have an update?"*

3. Sharing Your Work

- Reflex: *"Sorry this isn't perfect yet."*
- Rewrite: *"Here's the draft so far. Feedback is welcome."*

4. Running Late

- Reflex: *"Sorry I'm late, traffic was awful."*
- Rewrite: *"Thank you for your patience—I appreciate it."*

The difference is subtle but powerful. You're still polite. You're still collaborative. But you're no longer shrinking yourself with guilt that doesn't belong to you.

Meetings: Owning Your Space

Meetings are apology traps. Many people soften their voices with phrases like "Sorry, can I just add something?" or "Sorry if this is off-topic..."

Here are strategies for showing up differently:

1. Claim Your Contribution

Instead of asking permission to speak, claim your space:

- "I'd like to add something here."
- "From my perspective, one factor to consider is..."

2. State With Confidence

Even if you're unsure, present your ideas clearly:

- Reflex: *"Sorry, this might be a dumb question..."*
- Rewrite: *"Here's a question to help clarify..."*

3. Practice Body Language

Meetings aren't just about words—they're about presence. Sit upright, make eye contact, and resist shrinking postures (hunched shoulders, fiddling, covering your mouth). Your body can project confidence even when you don't feel it yet.

Case Story 1: Jamal in the Boardroom

Jamal worked in finance and dreaded weekly boardroom meetings. Every time he spoke, he prefaced his comments with: *"Sorry, just one thought..."*

His manager noticed and said: "You have great ideas, but you sound like you're asking for permission."

Jamal began practicing simple rewrites: instead of "Sorry, just one thought," he said: *"Here's one factor to consider."*

The shift was immediate. People stopped talking over him. His ideas landed. Within six months, Jamal was promoted—not because his ideas suddenly got better, but because he stopped apologizing for having them.

Emails: Polishing Your Digital Voice

Emails are one of the easiest places to spot the "sorry reflex"—and one of the easiest to fix.

Common culprits:

- "Sorry for the delay."
- "Sorry for the extra email."
- "Sorry to follow up."

Polished alternatives:

- "Thank you for your patience."
- "I appreciate your time on this."
- "I'm following up on the previous email."

Polished doesn't mean robotic. It means professional, clear, and respectful without layering guilt where it doesn't belong.

Case Story 2: Hannah's Inbox

Hannah was an HR coordinator who sent dozens of emails every day. She realized she was apologizing in almost every one: *"Sorry to bug you..." "Sorry if this is too much information..."*

She decided to audit her emails for one week. She highlighted every "sorry" and rewrote them before sending. At first, it felt stiff. But by the end of the week, her tone had transformed.

Her boss noticed. "Your emails sound so much more confident lately," he said. Hannah realized she hadn't just changed her inbox—she had changed her professional image.

Asking for Raises, Promotions, or Opportunities

Few things trigger the "sorry reflex" more than advocating for yourself at work. Many people start with hedges:

- *"Sorry to ask, but is there any chance I could be considered for..."*
- *"I know I probably don't deserve it yet, but..."*

This language weakens your case before it even begins. Instead, frame your request with clarity and confidence:

- "I'd like to discuss my growth here and opportunities for advancement."
- "Based on my contributions to [X project], I'd like to talk about adjusting my compensation."

You're not demanding. You're not apologizing. You're presenting facts.

Case Story 3: Rosa's Promotion

Rosa had been in the same role for five years. She wanted a promotion but always softened her requests: *"Sorry, I don't mean to be pushy, but do you think maybe I could..."*

84

When she finally decided to rewrite her script, she practiced this instead: *"I'd like to discuss my contributions this year and potential next steps for growth."*

Her manager listened. For the first time, Rosa sounded like she believed in herself. Within three months, she got the promotion she'd been waiting on for years.

Leadership Shifts: The Ripple Effect

If you're in a leadership role—or aspire to one—your language matters even more. Leaders who apologize reflexively risk undermining their authority, confusing their teams, and creating unnecessary tension.

This doesn't mean never apologizing. A sincere, well-timed apology from a leader is powerful. But constant sorrys erode trust. Teams want leaders who are clear, grounded, and accountable—not guilty.

A confident leader says:

- "I made a mistake. Here's how we'll fix it."
- "Thank you for your patience while we regroup."

An insecure leader says:

- "Sorry, I messed everything up, I'm the worst."

See the difference? One builds respect. The other builds pity.

Case Story 4: Marcus the Manager

Marcus was a new manager who apologized constantly to his team: *"Sorry I keep checking in, sorry I'm asking too much, sorry this process is so messy."*

One team member finally told him: "We don't need you to apologize—we need you to lead."

Marcus began reframing. Instead of *"Sorry this is messy,"* he said: *"Thanks for your patience while we figure this out together."* His team relaxed. Productivity improved. And Marcus realized: authority isn't about never messing up—it's about owning mistakes without drowning in guilt.

Exercises: Strengthening Workplace Confidence

1. The Email Audit

- Review your last 10 sent emails.
- Highlight every "sorry," "just," or "I think."
- Rewrite each one as if you could send it again.

2. Meeting Practice

- Before your next meeting, write down one point you'd like to make.
- Practice stating it out loud, without apology or hedging.
- In the meeting, speak it clearly. Afterwards, reflect: How did it land?

3. The Advocacy Script

- Write a script for asking for something you want—feedback, a raise, a project.
- Draft the reflex version (with apologies) and the confident version (without).
- Practice the confident version three times before your conversation.

The Bigger Picture: Respect Through Clarity

Apologies at work aren't just about language. They're about how you frame yourself in the professional world. Do you see yourself as someone who belongs, or as someone tiptoeing through the halls hoping not to upset anyone?

The truth is: you belong. Your contributions matter. And every time you strip away a reflexive sorry, you step more fully into your authority.

Closing Thought for Chapter 14

Workplace confidence isn't about arrogance. It's about clarity. It's about replacing apology with accountability, replacing guilt with gratitude, and replacing hedges with authority.

Every time you send an unapologetic email, every time you speak without shrinking in a meeting, every time you advocate for yourself without guilt—you build a new professional identity. One where your colleagues trust you, your bosses respect you, and most importantly, *you trust yourself.*

In the next chapter, we'll leave the office and head back into family life—because if apologies show up strongly at work, they often show up even more powerfully at home. And breaking free from unnecessary guilt in your family relationships may be the most liberating shift of all.

15

Family Dynamics

If the workplace is where we *perform* our apologies, family is often where we *learned* them. Long before emails and boardroom meetings, many of us were saying "sorry" at the dinner table, in sibling squabbles, or in tense moments with parents.

Family dynamics play a huge role in shaping how we use apology. Maybe you were the peacekeeper who smoothed over fights. Maybe you were the overachiever who apologized for never doing enough. Maybe you were told, *"Say you're sorry,"* even when you hadn't done anything wrong.

In this chapter, we'll explore how over-apologizing shows up in family life today—whether with parents, siblings, partners, or children—and how to start shifting those patterns. Because if you can change the way you communicate at home, you'll find it easier to change everywhere else.

The Family Roles That Breed Apologies

Every family system has roles, and often those roles dictate how and when you apologize.

- **The Peacekeeper:** Always smoothing conflict, saying sorry to keep the family calm—even if it wasn't your fault.
- **The Responsible One:** Apologizing when siblings misbehaved, because you felt it was your job to keep everything running.
- **The Invisible One:** Apologizing for existing, for needing attention, for taking up space.
- **The Performer:** Apologizing when you didn't make everyone laugh or keep things light.

These roles may have helped you survive childhood. But if you're still carrying them into adulthood, they can weigh heavily on your family relationships.

Parenting and Apology Cycles

Parenting is one of the most apology-laden roles in life. Many parents say "sorry" constantly to their kids:

- "Sorry, I burned dinner."
- "Sorry, I can't buy that toy."
- "Sorry, I yelled."

Some of these apologies are important—especially when they model accountability. But too many reflexive apologies can actually burden children. They may feel guilty for normal household stressors or start believing they're the cause of your unhappiness.

Reframe for Parents:

Instead of: *"Sorry I can't pick you up early."*

Try: *"Thank you for being flexible today. I'll see you after school."*

Instead of: *"Sorry I'm so stressed right now."*

Try: *"I'm having a hard day, but I love you and I'm glad you're here."*

This shift teaches kids that they are not the cause of your struggles—and that their role is not to absorb guilt, but to receive love.

Partners and the Weight of Sorry

In romantic relationships, "sorry" can become a shortcut. Instead of working through conflict, you throw out an apology to smooth things over. But too many hollow apologies can create resentment.

- You say sorry for needing rest, instead of honestly asking for help.
- You say sorry for being upset, instead of expressing the hurt underneath.
- You say sorry for not being perfect, instead of sharing your humanity.

Real intimacy doesn't come from endless apologies. It comes from honest conversations. Sometimes, *not apologizing* is the bravest thing you can do—because it forces you to show up with your real feelings instead of masking them with guilt.

Case Story 1: Anna and Her Mother

Anna grew up with a critical mother who often snapped, *"Say you're sorry!"* whenever conflict arose. By adulthood, Anna was apologizing for everything around her mother: moving too slowly, forgetting small things, even sighing too loudly.

One Thanksgiving, Anna decided to experiment. When her mother scolded her for not bringing the right dish, Anna felt the word "sorry" rise to her lips. Instead, she paused, breathed, and said: *"I thought this dish would be a nice addition. I hope you'll try it."*

Her mother frowned but moved on. For the first time, Anna realized: she didn't have to apologize for existing.

Case Story 2: Brian and His Teenage Son

Brian, a single dad, apologized constantly to his son: *"Sorry I work so much. Sorry I can't give you everything. Sorry I'm not around enough."*

His son finally said: "Dad, I don't need you to be sorry—I just want you to hang out with me when you can."

Brian realized his apologies weren't building closeness—they were creating distance. He began swapping "sorry" for presence: instead of apologizing for working late, he planned intentional time together. His son's response was immediate: less tension, more connection.

Case Story 3: Lila and Her Partner

Lila and her partner argued often about chores. Lila's reflex was to apologize before the conflict even unfolded: *"Sorry, I know I'm terrible at cleaning, sorry I always mess this up."*

Her partner grew frustrated. "I don't want your apologies—I want teamwork."

Lila practiced a rewrite. Instead of apologizing, she said: *"I see this is frustrating. Let's figure out a system that works better."*

It wasn't easy. Her heart raced every time she held back "sorry." But over time, their arguments became more productive. They stopped circling around guilt and started focusing on solutions.

Breaking the Family Apology Cycle

If you want to stop over-apologizing at home, you need to start by separating *real accountability* from *reflex guilt.*

1. Real Accountability

- Own it when you cause harm.
- Example: "I'm sorry I yelled. That wasn't fair to you. I'll work on handling stress differently."

2. Reflex Guilt

- Catch it when you apologize for things outside your control or for simply existing.
- Example: "Sorry I need some quiet." → Rewrite: "I'm going to take some quiet time."

3. Family Conversations

- Talk openly with your family about the shift. Let them know you're working on saying fewer unnecessary apologies, but that your love and accountability remain strong.

Exercises: Resetting Family Apologies

1. Family Audit
For one week, track every time you apologize in family interactions. Note whether each was real accountability or reflex guilt.

2. Rewrite With Gratitude
Choose one common reflex apology and swap it for thanks.

- "Sorry dinner is late" → "Thanks for waiting for dinner."

3. Partner/Child Feedback
Ask your partner or kids: "Do I apologize too much? How does it feel to you?" Their perspective may reveal patterns you don't see.

Why It Matters

Family is where the "sorry reflex" often begins—and it's also where it does the deepest damage if left unchecked. Reflexive apologies teach kids to carry guilt that isn't theirs. They turn intimacy into distance. They turn connection into performance.

But family is also the perfect place to practice change. If you can shift your words with the people closest to you, those changes ripple outward into every part of your life.

Closing Thought for Chapter 15

Family dynamics are powerful. They shape the way we see ourselves and how we move through the world. But they are not destiny. You don't have to carry the peacekeeper role forever. You don't have to apologize for being human.

When you stop over-apologizing at home, you create a family culture of honesty, gratitude, and respect. And in doing so, you give the people you love most the greatest gift: the real you.

In the next chapter, we'll explore another deeply personal space—friendships. Because while family teaches us early roles, friends often reinforce them in adulthood. And learning to stop apologizing with friends may be the bridge to living unapologetically everywhere.

16

Friendships Without Sorry

Friendships are supposed to be the safe places. The people you laugh with, cry with, call at midnight. Yet for many people who over-apologize, friendships become another arena where guilt and reflex apologies creep in.

You apologize for canceling plans, for not texting back quickly enough, for venting too long, for taking up space. And while the intention is to show care, too many apologies can actually weigh down the friendship. They can create imbalance, distance, or a sense that you don't believe you're truly welcome.

This chapter explores how the "sorry reflex" plays out in friendships, and how to replace it with honesty, gratitude, and presence—so your connections feel lighter, freer, and more authentic.

When Sorry Becomes the Third Wheel

Think of friendship as a conversation between two equals. When unnecessary apologies enter the mix, they act like a third wheel—always reminding one person that they're "too much" and the other that they need to reassure.

Common examples:

- "Sorry I've been such a bad friend."
- "Sorry I'm always venting."
- "Sorry I can't hang out more."
- "Sorry for talking too much."

At first, these apologies may feel like humility. But over time, they create a subtle imbalance: one person becomes the "burden" and the other the "comforter." Friendships thrive on mutuality, not constant guilt.

Gratitude Over Guilt

The most powerful swap in friendships is the same one you learned earlier: replacing "sorry" with "thank you."

- Instead of: *"Sorry I canceled."*
- Try: *"Thank you for understanding—I'll miss seeing you."*
- Instead of: *"Sorry I talk about myself too much."*
- Try: *"Thanks for listening—I really needed to share that."*
- Instead of: *"Sorry I didn't text back."*
- Try: *"Thanks for being patient—it means a lot."*

This small change shifts the friendship from imbalance to appreciation. Your friend doesn't walk away feeling like they had to carry your guilt. They walk away feeling valued.

Case Story 1: Priya and the Group Chat

Priya was part of a close-knit group of college friends who texted daily. Whenever she missed a conversation or forgot to reply, she sent: *"Sorry, I'm the worst friend."*

At first, her friends brushed it off. But over time, they grew weary of constantly reassuring her: *"You're not the worst!"* "Stop apologizing, we love you!"

One day, Priya tried something new. Instead of apologizing, she wrote: *"Thanks for keeping me in the loop even when I go quiet. I love how I can always come back and feel caught up."*

The tone shifted. Instead of feeling drained by guilt, her friends felt appreciated. The friendship lightened.

Case Story 2: Marcus and His Best Friend

Marcus had a best friend he'd known since childhood. Whenever they hung out, Marcus apologized for everything: being late, choosing the wrong restaurant, talking too much about work.

Finally, his friend said: "You don't need to say sorry every five minutes. I wouldn't be here if I didn't want to hang out."

That landed. Marcus realized his apologies weren't strengthening the friendship—they were eroding it. From then on, he practiced gratitude: *"Thanks for waiting." "Thanks for hearing me out."* Their time together became lighter and more fun, because Marcus wasn't dragging guilt into every interaction.

Case Story 3: Naomi and Her New Friends

Naomi had recently moved to a new city and was building friendships from scratch. Eager not to lose people, she over-apologized constantly: *"Sorry if I'm texting too much."* *"Sorry if I'm being clingy."*

One friend gently told her: "You don't need to apologize for wanting connection. That's why we're here."

Naomi realized her apologies were masking her fear of rejection. She started saying what she meant: *"I love texting with you—it makes me feel less lonely."* That honesty deepened her new friendships more than a dozen apologies ever could.

How Sorry Undermines Authenticity

In friendships, authenticity is everything. It's what makes a friend feel like *home.* But constant apologies erode that authenticity in three ways:

1. **They make you smaller.** Instead of showing up as yourself, you show up as a guilty version of yourself.
2. **They create imbalance.** Your friend is always the forgiver, you're always the "burden."
3. **They block intimacy.** True closeness comes from sharing real needs and feelings—not masking them with sorry.

Your friends don't want the apologetic version of you. They want *you.*

Exercises: Practicing Unapologetic Friendship

1. The Swap Challenge

For one week, every time you feel the urge to apologize in a friendship, swap it for gratitude.

- "Sorry I vented so much." → "Thanks for letting me vent."

2. The Honest Share

Practice naming your real need instead of apologizing for it.

- Instead of: "Sorry I'm being needy."
- Try: "I'd love to spend more time together this week."

3. The Guilt Journal

At the end of the day, jot down any friendship-related apologies you made or wanted to make. Ask: Was I apologizing for harm, or for existing? Rewrite each one as a statement of appreciation or honesty.

Friendship Is Not Transactional

One hidden reason people over-apologize in friendships is the belief that love is transactional: *If I inconvenience you, I owe you guilt.* But real friendship isn't a balance sheet. Your worth isn't measured in how little trouble you cause.

A true friend isn't keeping score of your "sorrys." They're showing up because they want *you*.

When you trust that, you can stop apologizing for canceled plans, for busy seasons, for needing to lean on them sometimes. You can simply show up, grateful and honest.

Closing Thought for Chapter 16

Friendship doesn't thrive on guilt. It thrives on honesty, appreciation, and presence. Every time you replace "sorry" with gratitude or real need, you deepen connection instead of weakening it.

Your friends don't need the self-erasing version of you. They need the version who says, *"Thank you for being here,"* and means it. The version who trusts that love isn't conditional on being perfect.

In the next chapter, we'll explore another deeply vulnerable arena—romantic relationships. Because while friendships can absorb some guilt, intimacy with a partner magnifies every apology. And learning to stop apologizing reflexively with someone you love may be the biggest test of all.

17

Romantic Relationships Without Sorry

If friendships can feel like a testing ground for the "sorry reflex," romantic relationships are where the habit often shows up in its most vulnerable form. When you love someone deeply— and rely on them for intimacy, support, and companionship— the stakes feel higher. Every disagreement feels scarier. Every request feels riskier. And "sorry" can slip in as a way to preserve connection at all costs.

But here's the paradox: in love, over-apologizing doesn't preserve intimacy—it erodes it. It creates imbalance, turns passion into performance, and makes honesty harder to find. This chapter will help you recognize how reflexive apologies shape your romantic relationships—and how to replace them with language that fosters respect, equality, and true closeness.

Why Love Feels Like the Danger Zone

Romantic relationships press all the nervous system's buttons. They combine attachment needs (safety, belonging, love) with vulnerability (fear of rejection, abandonment, criticism). For people prone to over-apologizing, that cocktail can trigger constant guilt.

- You apologize for being "too much."
- You apologize for not being enough.
- You apologize for needing time, attention, or reassurance.
- You apologize when you're emotional, angry, or upset.

These apologies are often less about real harm and more about fear: *If I'm difficult, you might stop loving me.*

It makes sense. If your earliest relationships taught you that love could be withdrawn when you caused conflict, your adult brain may see every disagreement as a threat to survival. "Sorry" becomes the shield you hold up to keep love from walking away.

The Hidden Cost of Sorry in Love

At first, apologizing can look like thoughtfulness: "I don't want to hurt you." But too many unnecessary apologies can actually create distance.

1. **It creates imbalance.** One partner becomes the guilty one, the other the forgiver. Equality fades.
2. **It masks true feelings.** Instead of saying, "I need more support," you say, "Sorry I'm so needy." The need gets buried.
3. **It erodes respect.** Over time, constant apologies can make one partner seem smaller, less confident, less attractive— not because they are, but because they show up that way.

Love thrives on honesty, not guilt. And that means learning to apologize when it matters—and stop apologizing when it doesn't.

Case Story 1: Ethan and the Date Nights

Ethan and his partner had an ongoing conflict about date nights. His partner wanted more quality time, but Ethan, swamped at work, often canceled. Every time, he'd say: *"Sorry, I'm the worst. I'm sorry, I'll make it up to you."*

At first, the apologies worked. His partner forgave him. But after a while, the words rang hollow. "I don't want your sorry," his partner said one night. "I want you to show up."

That hit Ethan hard. He realized his apologies weren't repairing—they were replacing action. From then on, Ethan stopped leading with "sorry" and started leading with account-ability: *"I didn't plan well. I'll reschedule, and I'll protect that night."* The shift rebuilt trust, because the apology wasn't reflex—it was paired with follow-through.

Case Story 2: Mariah and Her Emotions

Mariah often felt deeply emotional in her relationship. She cried easily, sometimes during arguments, sometimes just from stress. Every time, she blurted: *"I'm sorry I'm so sensitive. I'm sorry I'm like this."*

Her partner reassured her, but over time, Mariah noticed a distance. She realized her apologies were making her emotions seem like flaws to be excused instead of experiences to be shared.

One night, instead of saying sorry, she said: *"Thank you for sitting with me while I feel this. I know it's a lot sometimes, but it means so much that you stay."*

Her partner hugged her and said, "I don't want you to apologize for your feelings. I just want to understand them."

That moment changed things. Mariah realized that her emotions weren't a burden—her guilt was. When she replaced sorry with gratitude, intimacy deepened.

Case Story 3: Daniel and the Silence

Daniel hated conflict. Whenever he and his partner argued, he filled the silence with apologies: *"Sorry, sorry, you're right, I'll change."*

But his partner grew frustrated. "I don't want you to say sorry just to end the fight. I want to know what you actually think."

Daniel began practicing the pause. When he felt "sorry" rise in his throat, he took a breath and said, *"I need a minute to think."* It was awkward at first, but it gave space for real conversation. Instead of using apologies as a mask, Daniel learned to bring his authentic voice.

Shifting Apologies Into Authentic Communication

Here are ways to replace reflexive apologies in love with language that fosters respect and closeness:

1. Replace "sorry I'm needy" with honesty.

- Reflex: *"Sorry I always need reassurance."*
- Rewrite: *"I feel anxious sometimes, and hearing that you love me helps. Could you remind me?"*

2. Replace "sorry I got upset" with acknowledgment.

- Reflex: *"Sorry I'm so emotional."*
- Rewrite: *"I was hurt when that happened. I want to talk about it."*

3. Replace "sorry I'm difficult" with gratitude.

- Reflex: *"Sorry for being hard to live with."*
- Rewrite: *"Thank you for being patient while we figure this out together."*

Each swap removes guilt and adds either honesty, appreciation, or accountability—the three cornerstones of intimacy.

Exercises: Building Intimacy Without Guilt

1. The Partner Swap Challenge

- For one week, track when you apologize to your partner.
- Each time, ask: Was this a true apology (repairing harm) or a reflex apology (covering fear)?
- Practice swapping at least one reflex apology per day for honesty or gratitude.

2. The Vulnerability Practice

- Next time you feel tempted to say sorry for your emotions, pause.
- Instead of apologizing, name the feeling: *"I feel sad right now. I feel overwhelmed. I feel scared."*
- Notice how your partner responds when you bring feelings instead of guilt.

3. The Appreciation Ritual

- With your partner, create a nightly or weekly ritual of sharing one appreciation.
- This balances the relationship dynamic so that gratitude becomes the default language instead of apology.

The Deeper Truth: Love and Equality

At its core, love is about equality. Two people showing up as whole human beings, imperfect and real. Reflexive apologies disrupt that equality. They make one person the guilty one and the other the forgiver. They weaken the foundation of respect.

But when you stop apologizing for existing, you restore balance. You give your partner the gift of the real you—not the guilty version, but the honest, grateful, vulnerable version. And that version is far more lovable than any apology could ever be.

Closing Thought for Chapter 17

Romantic love doesn't need endless apologies to survive. It needs honesty, accountability, gratitude, and presence. When you replace reflexive guilt with authentic communication, you don't just preserve intimacy—you deepen it.

Your partner doesn't want a version of you that's always sorry. They want a version of you that's real, brave, and present. And that version is already inside you—waiting to speak without guilt.

In the next chapter, we'll look at one of the trickiest places to stop apologizing: public spaces and social interactions. Because if it feels hard to stop saying sorry to loved ones, it can feel downright impossible with strangers. But those everyday micro-apologies might be the very thing keeping you stuck.

18

Public Spaces & Social Interactions

Step into any crowded coffee shop, grocery store, or subway car, and you'll hear it: "Sorry, excuse me." "Sorry, can I squeeze past?" "Sorry, I didn't mean to take so long."

In public and social settings, "sorry" can become the sound-track of your day. We say it to strangers, acquaintances, service workers, even people who bump into *us*. And while politeness matters, many of these apologies aren't really about kindness. They're about shrinking—sending the message, *I'm not a bother, please don't be mad at me for existing.*

This chapter explores how unnecessary apologies play out in public and social spaces, and how to replace them with language that is polite, respectful, and confident—without layering guilt on top of everyday human interactions.

Why Strangers Trigger Sorry

It might feel strange to think about apologizing to people you don't even know, but it makes sense. Public spaces can feel like stages. You're aware of being observed. You don't want to seem rude, clumsy, or in the way.

For people with a strong "sorry reflex," strangers trigger the same nervous system response as loved ones: a flash of fear that you'll upset someone or be judged. The result? Apologies spill out for things that don't require them at all:

- Apologizing when someone bumps into you.
- Apologizing for asking a cashier to double-bag your groceries.
- Apologizing for ordering slowly at a coffee shop.

These aren't moments of wrongdoing. They're moments of being human. But "sorry" slips in to soften your presence.

Politeness vs. Apology

It's important to distinguish between kindness and apology. You *can* be polite, considerate, and respectful without being reflexively sorry.

Polite alternatives to reflexive sorry include:

- "Excuse me."
- "Thanks for your patience."
- "Go ahead."
- "Appreciate it."

Notice how each one communicates respect without self-erasure. You're acknowledging others while still standing in your own worth.

Case Story 1: Leah on the Subway

Leah commuted daily by subway in New York. Packed trains made her anxious, and she apologized constantly: "Sorry, sorry, sorry," as she squeezed past people.

One day, she decided to swap "sorry" for "excuse me." At first, it felt bold. But she noticed something surprising: people responded better. They moved aside, nodded, and even said "sure." Nobody looked offended.

Leah realized she hadn't been apologizing for bumping people—she'd been apologizing for existing in the space. Swapping to "excuse me" helped her take up room without guilt.

Case Story 2: Thomas at the Café

Thomas loved his neighborhood café, but ordering gave him anxiety. He always said, "Sorry, I'll be quick," when it was his turn—sometimes before he even looked at the menu.

One morning, he tried a swap: *"Thanks for waiting—I'll take a moment to decide."*

The barista smiled and said, "Take your time."

Thomas realized that he'd been apologizing not because he was slow, but because he felt unworthy of holding space. Gratitude changed the energy—for him and for the people around him.

Case Story 3: Rosa at the Grocery Store

Rosa apologized constantly while grocery shopping: "Sorry, let me grab this." "Sorry, I'm in your way." "Sorry, sorry, sorry."

She decided to do a one-week experiment. Instead of apologizing, she tried: *"Excuse me," "Thanks,"* or simply standing her ground with a smile.

At first, it felt terrifying. But to her surprise, no one scolded her. Most people responded politely. And Rosa discovered something profound: she wasn't as "in the way" as she thought. Her guilt was louder than reality.

The Social Layer: Parties, Networking, Small Talk

It's not just strangers—social interactions with acquaintances can be apology minefields too.

- You apologize for arriving late: *"Sorry I'm always a mess."*
- You apologize for leaving early: *"Sorry I'm such a party pooper."*
- You apologize for speaking up: *"Sorry if I'm boring everyone."*

In reality, most people aren't keeping score. They're glad you showed up. They're glad you joined the conversation. The apologies aren't helping—they're making you appear less confident and more self-critical than you really are.

Confidence shifts for social settings:

- Arriving late? → "Thanks for waiting—I'm glad to be here."
- Leaving early? → "It's been great—looking forward to next time."

- Speaking up? → "Here's my thought…"

Exercises: Reclaiming Public Space Without Sorry

1. The Subway/Store Experiment

- For one week, track how often you say "sorry" to strangers.
- Swap each one for "excuse me" or "thank you."
- Reflect: How did people respond? How did you feel?

2. The Social Swap Game

- At your next party, networking event, or casual gathering, challenge yourself to make it through without one reflexive apology.
- Replace each with gratitude ("Thanks for including me") or presence ("It's good to see you").

3. The Worthy Presence Affirmation

- Before entering a public space, repeat: *"I'm allowed to take up space here. My presence isn't a problem."*
- Notice how this affects your posture, tone, and urge to apologize.

The Bigger Picture: Owning Your Space in the World

Public spaces are where the "sorry reflex" reveals its full reach. Every unnecessary apology says: *I don't belong here. I'm in the way. I'm a problem.*

But you are not a problem. You are a person, moving through

the world like everyone else. By shifting your language—from "sorry" to "excuse me," from guilt to gratitude—you teach yourself and others that your presence is normal, valid, and worthy.

Closing Thought for Chapter 18

Confidence isn't just built in boardrooms or therapy offices—it's built in grocery aisles, subway cars, and coffee shops. Every time you swap "sorry" for gratitude or politeness without guilt, you're retraining your nervous system. You're teaching yourself: *I belong here. I'm not a burden. I can move through the world unapologetically.*

In the next chapter, we'll zoom out even further—to look at culture and society. Because while your "sorry reflex" feels personal, it's also shaped by the messages you've absorbed from the world around you. And understanding those cultural forces can help you finally let go of guilt that never belonged to you in the first place.

19

Culture & Society

If you've ever wondered why your "sorry reflex" runs so deep, the answer isn't just personal—it's cultural. While families shape early habits, society at large often reinforces them. The messages you've absorbed about politeness, gender, race, class, and power all influence how freely you speak and how often you apologize.

This chapter explores the bigger picture: how culture and society condition people into over-apologizing, how those forces show up in daily life, and how you can begin separating *your voice* from *the voice of expectation*.

The Culture of Politeness

Many societies equate politeness with apology. From a young age, you're taught:

- *"Say you're sorry to Grandma."*
- *"Apologize for interrupting."*
- *"Be nice. Don't cause trouble."*

These lessons aren't inherently bad—teaching kids empathy matters. But often, the nuance gets lost. Apology becomes less about repairing harm and more about keeping everyone else comfortable.

By adulthood, politeness and guilt feel interchangeable. Asking for what you need feels impolite. Saying no feels selfish. Having boundaries feels rude. And "sorry" becomes the shortcut to soften every edge of your humanity.

Gender and the Sorry Reflex

Research shows that women apologize more frequently than men—not because women do more wrong, but because women are socialized to interpret more behaviors as "wrong."

- A woman says sorry for speaking up in a meeting.
- A man says his piece without apology.
- A woman says sorry for being late, even by one minute.
- A man arrives late and says, "Thanks for waiting."

This isn't about blaming individuals—it's about conditioning. Women are often rewarded for being agreeable, accommodating, and self-effacing, while men are rewarded for being assertive.

But this isn't limited to gender. Cultural expectations play out across race, class, sexuality, and beyond. People from marginalized groups may feel extra pressure to apologize for taking up space in systems not built for them.

The Weight of Power Dynamics

Apology is also shaped by power. You may apologize more often around authority figures—bosses, teachers, doctors—because society trains us to equate hierarchy with permission.

Think about these common moments:

- Apologizing for asking a doctor to clarify something.
- Apologizing for emailing a professor with a question.
- Apologizing to a boss for needing time off, even though it's your right.

These reflex apologies aren't about personal guilt. They're about centuries of cultural conditioning that equate authority with dominance and self-advocacy with rudeness.

Case Story 1: Mei in the Office

Mei was raised in a culture that emphasized harmony and respect for authority. At work in the U.S., she apologized constantly to her boss: *"Sorry to bother you, sorry for asking, sorry this isn't perfect."*

Her boss finally said: "Mei, you don't need to be sorry— you're doing great."

That feedback startled her. Mei realized her apologies weren't reflecting her performance—they were reflecting cultural habits. With coaching, she began replacing "sorry" with "thank you" and "I'd like." Over time, she noticed her boss taking her more seriously.

Case Story 2: Carlos at Family Gatherings

Carlos grew up in a family where men didn't show emotion. Any time he expressed sadness or frustration, he apologized: *"Sorry, I'm being weak."*

But in his adult friendships, he began to notice something. When he shared feelings without apology, his friends leaned in. They didn't think he was weak—they thought he was honest.

Carlos realized his "sorry reflex" wasn't really his voice. It was society's script, telling him masculinity meant silence. Rewriting that script allowed him to show up more fully in his relationships.

Case Story 3: Aisha in Customer Service

Aisha worked in retail and found herself apologizing to customers constantly—even when the issue wasn't her fault. Out-of-stock product? "Sorry." Long lines? "Sorry." A rude customer? "Sorry."

One day, a coworker pointed out: "You're apologizing for things beyond your control. You don't need to carry all that."

Aisha practiced swapping "sorry" for empathy without guilt: *"Thank you for your patience"* or *"I know it's frustrating when things run out."* She noticed customers actually responded better—they felt seen, not burdened with her guilt.

How to Separate Conditioning from Choice

Awareness is the first step. Once you see that many of your apologies come from cultural scripts, you can begin to choose differently.

1. Question the Rule

· When you feel the urge to apologize, ask: *Who taught me I need to say sorry here? Was it family, culture, society? Do I actually agree?*

2. Reclaim the Script

· Write down three apologies you often say. Next to each, write: *Is this my authentic belief, or someone else's expectation?*

3. Practice Public Neutrality

· Try one week of moving through public interactions without unnecessary apologies. Notice how often the world still accepts you, even without guilt.

Exercises: Cultural Awareness Practice

1. The Socialization Journal

· Write about the earliest memory you have of being told to apologize.
· Reflect: Did it teach you accountability—or people-pleasing?

2. The Role Reversal

· Imagine someone else in your shoes (your brother, your coworker, your boss). Would they apologize in the same situation? If not, why do you feel you must?

3. The Conditioning Check-In

- Each time you catch yourself apologizing, ask: *Is this me—or my conditioning?*
- Over time, the line will become clearer.

The Bigger Picture: From Reflex to Resistance

When you recognize the cultural roots of the "sorry reflex," something shifts. You realize it's not just a personal flaw—it's a learned survival mechanism, reinforced by society. And every time you resist it, you're not just freeing yourself—you're quietly resisting the forces that told you to shrink in the first place.

Refusing to apologize unnecessarily becomes an act of empowerment. It's not about arrogance. It's about saying: *I belong. I don't need to carry guilt that isn't mine. I am allowed to take up space.*

Closing Thought for Chapter 19

Culture teaches us many things. Some are beautiful—like empathy, kindness, and respect. Others weigh us down—like guilt, silence, and self-erasure.

The work of unlearning isn't about rejecting your culture. It's about choosing which lessons serve you and which no longer do. When you stop apologizing for expectations you didn't choose, you make room for authenticity. And authenticity is the deepest form of confidence.

In the next chapter, we'll bring it all together by looking at resilience—the ability to slip, stumble, or even fall back into old apology habits without shaming yourself. Because progress isn't about perfection—it's about persistence.

20

Resilience & Relapse

By now, you've practiced spotting your "sorry reflex," swapping it for gratitude, rewriting scripts, calming your nervous system, and even reshaping how you show up in family, work, and public spaces. You've begun to untangle the cultural scripts that taught you to apologize for existing.

But here's the reality: you're still going to slip. You're still going to say "sorry" without meaning to. You'll still catch yourself defaulting to old scripts in stressful moments. And that's not failure—it's part of the process.

This final chapter is about resilience. It's about learning to expect relapses, embrace imperfection, and keep practicing without letting guilt pull you backward.

Why Relapse Happens

Apologies are habits built over years—sometimes decades. They're stored not only in your vocabulary, but in your nervous system. So of course, they won't vanish in a few weeks.

Relapse happens because:

- **Stress resets old habits.** When you're tired, overwhelmed, or scared, your brain falls back on familiar coping strategies.
- **Certain relationships trigger deeper patterns.** Around parents, bosses, or partners, your childhood scripts may resurface more strongly.
- **Perfectionism sneaks in.** You might think, *If I apologize once, I've failed.* That belief can push you back into shame, which ironically leads to more apologies.

Relapse is not a sign you can't change. It's proof that you're human.

Reframing Relapse as Practice

Imagine you're learning guitar. You don't pick it up once and play flawlessly. You practice, fumble, repeat. Each mistake strengthens your muscle memory.

Changing apology habits works the same way. Every relapse is a practice opportunity. Each time you catch yourself saying sorry unnecessarily, you're building awareness. Each time you rewrite the apology afterward—even just in your head—you're training new neural pathways.

Relapse isn't a setback. It's part of progress.

Case Story 1: Hannah at the Staff Meeting

Hannah had been practicing unapologetic language for months. But one stressful Monday, she reverted. In a single staff meeting, she apologized six times: *"Sorry, I know I'm rambling." "Sorry for interrupting." "Sorry if this is a dumb question."*

Afterward, she felt defeated. *All that practice, and I blew it.*

But instead of giving up, she used it as data. She asked herself: *What triggered me today?* The answer: she felt insecure in front of a new boss.

Armed with that insight, Hannah prepped extra for her next meeting and practiced clear, confident openings. The following week, she apologized only once. Progress—not perfection.

Case Story 2: David with His Parents

David had stopped apologizing unnecessarily at work, but when he visited his parents, the old reflex roared back. He apologized for eating too much, for resting on the couch, for speaking his mind.

At first, he felt ashamed. *Why can't I be the confident version of myself here?*

Then he realized: these were childhood triggers. His nervous system was remembering old roles. Instead of scolding himself, David showed compassion: *Of course this is harder here. I'm practicing decades of unlearning.*

That mindset shift helped. Slowly, he began experimenting with gratitude instead of guilt around his parents. Change came slower—but it came.

Case Story 3: Sofia at the Dinner Party

Sofia had sworn off reflex apologies. But at a dinner party, she laughed too loudly and instantly blurted: *"Sorry, I'm being obnoxious."*

Her friend smiled and said: "You don't need to apologize—you're fun."

Sofia caught herself. Instead of spiraling into shame, she

laughed and said: *"Thank you for letting me be myself."*

That tiny reframe turned a relapse into a moment of connection.

Tools for Resilience

1. Catch & Correct

- When you apologize unnecessarily, don't beat yourself up. Simply pause and correct.
- Example: "Sorry I'm late." → "Actually, thank you for waiting."

2. Debrief, Don't Dwell

- Instead of ruminating on every apology, ask: *What triggered me? How can I prep for next time?*
- Turn guilt into growth.

3. Build a Relapse Plan

- Expect slips. Have a mantra ready: *Progress, not perfection.*
- Or: *This is practice, not failure.*

The Role of Self-Compassion

If over-apologizing is rooted in guilt, then the antidote is self-compassion. You cannot guilt yourself out of guilt—you can only love yourself out of it.

Self-compassion sounds like:

- "I slipped today, but I'm still learning."
- "I apologized more than I wanted, but I noticed—that's progress."
- "I deserve patience, the same way I give it to others."

Compassion keeps you moving forward, while shame keeps you stuck.

Exercises: Building Resilience

1. The Relapse Journal

- Each time you relapse, jot it down.
- Note: What triggered it? How did I respond? What could I try next time?

2. The Self-Compassion Letter

- Write a letter to yourself as if you were your best friend.
- Example: "Hey, you had a tough day. You slipped, but you're still learning. I'm proud of you."

3. The "Next Time" Rehearsal

- After a relapse, rewrite the script.
- Example: You said, "Sorry I talked too much." Rehearse: "Thanks for letting me share."

Closing the Loop: Progress, Not Perfection

Breaking the "sorry reflex" isn't about never apologizing again. It's about building awareness, choice, and confidence. It's about using apologies for repair—not reflex. It's about learning to stand in your worth without shrinking.

And it's about practicing resilience. You'll slip. You'll relapse. But each time you catch yourself, each time you reframe, you're rewiring your brain, your body, and your relationships.

Remember: you're not aiming for perfection. You're aiming for freedom. The freedom to speak clearly, to take up space, to show up authentically—without guilt weighing you down.

So when you hear yourself say sorry unnecessarily tomorrow, don't panic. Smile. You just caught yourself in the act of transformation.

Final Words

This book began with a simple question: *Why do I say sorry all the time?* Along the way, you've discovered that it's not weakness—it's survival. It's not personality—it's conditioning. And it's not permanent—it's changeable.

Now, you hold the tools:

- Awareness of your triggers.
- Swaps for gratitude and clarity.
- Scripts for work, family, friendships, and love.
- Nervous system resets to stay calm.
- And resilience to keep going when you slip.

Your journey to unapologetic living doesn't end here. It begins now—with every word, every pause, every moment of courage.

Because the truth is simple: you don't have to apologize for being human. You only have to live it.

21

Conclusion

Living Unapologetically

When we began this journey together, I asked if you ever caught yourself apologizing for things that weren't your fault—apologizing for being late, for needing help, for taking up space. Maybe you recognized yourself in those stories. Maybe you saw how "sorry" had become a shield—something you carried out of habit, safety, or fear.

Along the way, we uncovered the truth: over-apologizing isn't weakness. It's not a flaw in your character. It's a survival strategy, learned in childhood, reinforced by culture, and carried into every corner of life. And most importantly—it's changeable.

You've learned how to swap "sorry" for gratitude, how to rewrite scripts, how to set boundaries without guilt, how to calm your nervous system, and how to show up with confidence at work, at home, with friends, in love, and in public spaces. You've seen that relapse is part of the process—and that resilience, not perfection, is what transforms you.

But the biggest lesson is this: you don't need to apologize for existing. You don't need to shrink to be loved. You don't need to erase yourself to be accepted. Your voice, your needs, your presence—they belong.

As you step forward, I hope you carry three anchors:

- **Awareness:** Notice the reflex. Awareness is the first crack in the old habit.
- **Choice:** Swap guilt for gratitude, apology for honesty, reflex for presence.
- **Compassion:** When you slip, meet yourself with kindness. This is how change lasts.

You will still say "sorry" sometimes. And that's okay. The goal isn't to banish the word forever—it's to use it intentionally, when repair is needed, not reflexively, when you simply exist.

So here's your invitation: live unapologetically. Speak with clarity. Take up space. Offer gratitude. Set boundaries. Be seen.

The world doesn't need the smaller, apologetic version of you. It needs the real you—present, confident, and free.

Because your life is too important to live it through "sorry."

✧ That gives your book a strong, uplifting close that mirrors the energy of your introduction but with a sense of resolution and empowerment.

About the Author

James Douglas is a writer and researcher based in Nashville, Tennessee. He enjoys exploring topics like artificial intelligence, fitness, and personal growth, with a focus on making complex ideas practical and accessible. James also writes books fueled by personal passion, aiming to inspire and empower readers in every season of life.

Printed in Dunstable, United Kingdom